Understanding Asian Mission Movements

Understanding Asian Mission Movements

Proceedings of the
Asian Mission Consultations
held at Redcliffe College, Gloucester
2008–2010

Edited by
Kang San Tan
Jonathan Ingleby
Simon Cozens

Wide Margin

Published in 2011 by Wide Margin,
90 Sandyleaze, Gloucester, GL2 0PX, UK

http://www.wide-margin.co.uk/

ISBN 978-0-9565943-8-9

Printed and bound in Great Britain by
Lightning Source, Milton Keynes

Contents

Introduction

Jonathan Ingleby

One hundred years ago, Western Europe sent three hundred times more missionaries than the whole of Asia. Today, the numbers are roughly equal.[1] Korea is currently the second largest missionary sending country in the world, and has consistently added thousands of missionaries to the world mission force over the past five years. In the next ten years, we can expect Asia to move from being a net receiver of missionaries to becoming a net sender.

The rise of Asian mission poses important questions to the global Church: How can we best relate to these burgeoning Asian mission movements? What can we learn from them? What models of partnership, mutual support and resourcing are appropriate—on both sides?

The three Asian Mission Consultations held at Redcliffe College in Gloucester between 2008 and 2010 brought together mission leaders and practitioners from Asian and non-Asian missions to interact with these questions, around the following themes:

2008: Growing Asian Mission Movements: Issues and Models for Partnership

---

1 Johnson, Todd M., David B. Barrett, and Peter F. Crossing, "Christianity 2010: A View from the New *Atlas of Global Christianity*", *International Bulletin of Missionary Research*, 34:1, 2010.

2009: Asian Mission Movements: Competition or Collaboration?

2010: Resourcing and Equipping Asian Mission

This book comprises the papers read, presented and discussed at the three conferences. My thanks to all the authors of the papers and the conference delegates; to Redcliffe College for hosting and supporting the conference; to the other sponsors of the conference, OMF, Wycliffe, CMS, Faith2Share, Global Connections; and to the Asian Mission Consultation Committee members, Anton Ponomarev, Ann Bower, Hun Kim, David Pickard, Loun Lin Tan, and especially to Kang San Tan for initiating and supporting this book project.

What are the main missiological themes that emerge from the three conferences that contribute papers to this book? I have tried to put these as a series of questions, and as one contributor says, it may be that at this stage the questions are more important than the answers.

What about the big scene? How does Asia fit into the world picture? It is increasingly obvious that we simply cannot ignore Asia when assessing the global scene. China and India are the world's two most populous nations and the Chinese and Indian diasporas have a worldwide significance. Japan and the Asian Tigers have long excelled in terms of economic performance, and China and India are rapidly becoming two new economic super-powers. With economic success comes political clout. In terms of religion, Asia is the most complex of all the continents.

But what about mission within and from Asian countries and from nation to nation within the region? There is much to be said about this. The Korean mission force, for example, is now the second largest in the world. India has long set an example of successful cross cultural mission both within the nation's borders and beyond. These are but two examples.

The rise of Asian Mission Movements (AMMs) raises some crucial questions about partnership with the older missions from the West. Are Western missions ready for such partnership and is it going to be genuine, or will they insist on trying to retain the unchallenged power they once had? Are AAMs reproducing the mistakes already made by Western missions? Some of our Asian contributors suggest that this might be the case. Would it be better, at least for the time being, for the new Asian missions to go their own way and to learn from their own mistakes? In fact is 'going their own way' possible in a globalised world? What are the new insights, in terms of missiology, that the AAMs can bring to the table? Is anybody listening? Can we begin to forget the old 'us' and 'them'—an attitude which the very word 'partnership' may inadvertently promote – and find a genuinely global and postcolonial way of advancing together?

Several papers take a long hard look at this theme of partnership. It is clearly an issue that will not quickly go away. Here it receives theological reflection, historical analysis and above all consideration of the practical issues, with numerous very helpful, real life, examples. My own feeling is that we have got to go on working hard at partnership while at the same time thinking about new ways of looking at mission from a global and postcolonial perspective, as I mention above.

What about history? One wonders sometimes whether AMMs are in such a hurry to go on to the next thing that they find it difficult to listen to the past. The mission history of Asia needs much more attention, particularly from Asian scholars. The best secular history begs to be matched by mission history of an equivalent standard. There is so much on which to reflect. Just to take a couple of examples, the life of a great missionary statesman like Lesslie Newbigin provides a whole set of lessons, while the sad mixture of colonialism and mission in the years before Asian independence (not easily forgotten by Asians to this day) provide another.

What about context? We are reminded how key the socio-political context can be in mission (the Korean versus the Japanese experience, for example). We certainly need wise Asian leaders to interpret the signs of the times. These papers provide some commentary of this sort but much more is needed.

The movement of peoples is an important aspect of the contemporary context. There is a brilliant description in one of the papers of the way that millions of Chinese workers move about in their own country. Many of them are crowding into cities as urban life becomes more and more the typical Asian context, another theme dealt with by one of our contributors. Then there is the interest in diaspora people who are increasingly seen both as potential evangelists and ripe for evangelism.

Money is always an issue. Are declining finances a threat or an opportunity? (Something which has become a global issue since the financial crash in 2008.) But there are other questions. The problems of affluence are also many, as one contributor points out, thinking particularly of the threat to local identities and cultures because of globalisation. More money for missions also has its problems. Going from a relatively well-to-do nation to a poorer one quickly leads to an unconscious cultural superiority.

The issue of training is particularly urgent. Of course it is encouraging to hear of Asian mission to the West, but urgent questions arise about preparation and cultural awareness—the same questions that still arise when Western missionaries are coming to Asia. Are any of us being adequately prepared for the shock of a rapidly globalising world and an increasingly influential postmodernism, the latter now the cultural norm of most Westerners?

At least one paper speaks about the church and the need for a new ecclesiology instead of more mission agencies. It raises the question as to whether the Western model of mission agencies as the chief spearhead of missionary endeavour is the right one. Another paper notes that for Korean missionaries, for example, the relationship between their home churches and the churches they have planted is often a complicated one.

What about methods? One paper makes a strong plea for a revival of Christian apologetic but also hints that a successful method in one context might fail in another. Korean missionaries have been predominantly church planters. Is this still the best way forward? The much debated issue to do with the relationship between evangelism and social action still needs further thought in the context of Asian missions.

Finally, what about Asian religions? It is notable that Christian mission from the West has had very little success in impacting the main Asian religions. Will AMMs fare any better? It is also notable that though one paper calls for 'a dialogue between major religious traditions', none of our papers really tackle the issue! Perhaps we urgently need another conference on this subject.

The papers in this book begin to look at some of the issues that I have highlighted in this introduction—Asia's place in today's world, Asian Mission Movements, partnership, Asian mission history, contextual awareness, people movements, money , training, ecclesiology, missionary methods, Asian religions. Reading about these complex and vital issues will, it is hoped, encourage all of us who care about Asian mission to get into the action.

Action, of course, does not just mean 'doing'; it includes thinking harder, discussing more openly, seeing more clearly.

China and Beyond: Issues, Trends and Opportunities

Patrick Fung

An unexpected challenge—a devastating snowstorm

With high hopes for the Beijing Olympics, China started 2008 facing the worst winter weather in more than 50 years. Snow and ice had crushed houses, brought down power lines and crippled transportation across a wide swath of 10 provinces in central China. Hundreds of thousands became homeless. Millions were affected.

Culture joined forces with climate to compound the suffering. The Lunar New Year season witnesses the greatest migration of people on earth every year. This year, an estimated 10% of China's population, i.e. 120 million people headed home for the Lunar New Year. Worst hit were the *min-gong*—migrant workers—millions of them from the poorer western provinces, employed in the eastern and southern seaboard factories producing 'Made in China' goods for the business markets around the world. With train services unpredictable due to atrocious weather and millions on the move, railway stations became crushing masses of humanity.

During this time, as many as 800,000 travellers jammed around Guangzhou (Canton) railway station. They could not make it home for the Lunar New Year family get-together, but their factory dormitories were closed for the holidays. Wen Jiabao, 'The People's Premier', visited the worst hit areas, urging calm, patience and hope, while calling on local leaders and factory owners to do all they could to alleviate the suffering.

What characterizes China is people, masses of people.

The study of Chinese people has always been challenging. Even though early researchers were aware that China had a large number of different tribes and peoples, there was generally no systematic approach to gather biographical data in the early 20th century. Some of the most influential research was a survey published by John Kuhn, a well known China Inland Mission missionary, who documented 100 tribes in the Yunnan Province in 1944.

Everywhere we kept finding tribes, many of whom we had never heard of, until our hearts were thrilled. On December 23 we tabulated the one-hundredth tribe! One hundred tribes in Yunnan! And two-thirds of these had never had a gospel witness.

In 1953, over 400 minority groups were submitted to the Chinese government for recognition, of which 260 came from Yunnan Province alone. Since then many revisions have been carried out. In 1976, the State Council of the People's Republic confirmed 55 officially recognized minorities, comprising nearly 10% of China's population. Some of the largest minority groups include the Zhuang[1] (18m), Hui (10m), Tibetans (5m), Yi (8m), Uygur[2] (9m).

An unexpected joy—printing of 50 million Bibles

For many years, one of the greatest needs of the church in China was the supply of Bibles, the Word of God. Older believers still keep hand-copied Bibles which were very common in the 60s and 70s. However, Amity Press based in Nanjing celebrated recently the printing of 50 millions Bibles in China so far. The Amity Press, located in a 85,000 square-metre factory, in Nanjing, Jiangsu province, caters to the mainland's growing thirst for Christianity. It was only in 1988 that Amity began its first full year of production with half a million Bibles printed. By 2009 it will supply an estimated 25% of the world's new Bibles—and most will be for domestic use.

Amity is a partnership between a Chinese Christian charity and the United Bible Societies (UBS). Of the 50 million Bibles Amity has printed so far, 80% of them, Chinese-language editions, are sold through official

1   The Zhuang are China's largest minority. The Zhuang are animists and ancestor worshippers. In 2002 scholars claimed to have discovered the birthplace of Buluotuo, the very first Zhuang. This has resulted in a revival of Zhuang culture and a renewed interest in ancient Zhuang religious texts.

2   Paul Hattaway, *Operation China*, Carlisle: Piquant, 2000.

churches within the mainland for as little as 10 Yuan (Chinese dollar) a Bible[3]. Though a non-religious or non-church organization, Amity has done something remarkable for Christians in China. The factory, with a 600-strong workforce of mostly non-Christian locals, is printing Bible in 90 languages, ranging from Slovakian to a broad variety of African dialects as well as 7 Chinese minority languages, including Lagu, Miao, and Yi.[4]

The Director General of China State Administration for Religious Affairs, Minister Ye Xiaowen, made the announcement on Dec 8 2007 in Nanjing that "Bibles printed by the Amity Printing Company (APC) will be provided to participants in the 2008 Olympic Games in Beijing."[5]

With so many Chinese Bibles printed, one may wonder where are all these Bibles going? There are 55,000 state-registered Protestant churches in China and at least 4 times as many house churches. The number of Christians in China is estimated to be between 50 million to 100 million. Certainly, the church in China is alive and growing.

The Chinese Christian Council is also preparing for the Olympics. It has commissioned a special edition of the gospel of Mark with Han Duan's picture on the cover in preparation for the 2008 Olympics. She is a member of China's Women's National Football team and is a Christian.

3   South China Morning Post- Post Magazine Nov 25 2007. p. 28.

4   David Aikman, *Jesus in Beijing*, Washington: Regnery Publishing, Inc., 2003.

5   United Bible Society Newsletter 466, Dec 13, 2007.

The 2008 Olympic Games are scheduled to begin precisely at 8:08pm on August 8, 2008. The Number "8" theme is of course chosen with special intent. It is a number symbolizing hope and prosperity in the Chinese culture. A big digital clock was placed at Tiananmen Square showing the count down to the start of the games.

If we turn back our clock 200 hundred years, Robert Morrison, the first Protestant missionary to China, arrived in Canton on September 8th, 1807. As a matter of fact, the East India Company refused Robert Morrison passage on any of their ships bound for China or accommodation upon arrival, fearing that he would interfere with their unconscionable opium trade. Morrison set out on his mission of love, knowing full well he could not succeed alone. "Do you really expect that you can make an impression on the great Chinese empire?" a U.S. shipping agent asked him. "No, Sir. I expect God will," he said.

As a trailblazer, Morrison spearheaded landmark work that others would benefit from and build on. He not only compiled the first Chinese-English dictionary but during his first 12 years in China, with the help of local scholars, Morrison also translated and published the first complete edition of the Bible in Chinese.[6] This was no small undertaking: no one had undertaken such an effort since the time Nestorian monks first came to China with the gospel 1200 years earlier.

6   "A Call to Christian Professionals"- MSI regular bulletin, Issue 48, 2007.

While the overseas Chinese churches commemorated the 200th anniversary of Morrison's arrival in China with excitement and celebration, the official church in China did not demonstrate the same enthusiasm. A special symposium, entitled, "Symposium on the Missionary Movement and the Chinese Church" was held in Shanghai in November 2006, ahead of the Robert Morrison 200th year anniversary celebration. The conference was organized by the CCC/TSPM. Participants included church historians, scholars, university professors and research specialists, altogether 150. It is important to pay attention to the speech by the President of the Chinese Christian Council, Rev. Cao Shengjie, who presided over the closing ceremony. He emphasized again the importance of the three self principles, i.e. self-supporting, self-management and self-propagation. He commented that when Christianity first entered China, missionaries advocated that the Christian faith should replace or transform the Chinese culture. As a result, the Chinese church ideology and theology struck a "discordant note" with the Chinese society. He stressed that the Chinese church should take root in the Chinese culture and re-construct its own theological system.

Several important papers were presented at the conference. The strongest criticism of the early missionaries to China was the close connection between missionaries and companies that were involved in the opium trade.[7] Even looking at some of the early missionaries who were involved in medical work, including Dr. Peter Parker, the first medical missionary to

7   Report on the "Symposium of the Missionary Movement and the Chinese Church" Jan 5 2007
http://www.chineseprotestantchurch.org/ Chinese edition.

China in the past 200 years, we see many were also key interpreters and negotiators for foreign governments in negotiating treaties with Chinese counterpart. This was partly because of their excellent language acquisition. Though most missionaries in those days vigorously criticized the opium traffic, very few however seemed serious enough to challenge the right of the British to compel China to open her doors. China was forced to give special privileges to missionaries obtained by force of arms of foreign nations. The opium trade, the opium war, the unequal treaties, particularly the treaty of Nanjing in 1842, made it harder for many Chinese to appreciate the love of Christ that had motivated many of these trailblazers including Morrison's perseverance and sacrifice.

The challenge of the Olympics

"One World, One dream" was the theme of the 2008 Beijing Olympic games. China certainly hopes that the Olympics will be a catalyst to continue its surge as an economic and global power. China is certainly going to show the world that she can do it.

To mark the seriousness of preparation for the Beijing Olympics, a panel of 13 specialists from the China Meteorological Administration, the Beijing emergency commission office, and other relevant units convened on October 19th 2007 to review the analysis of the potential meteorological disasters and hazards during the Beijing Olympic Games. The report included a study on the potential sources of weather-related disasters and hazards during the Games, an evaluation of these potential hazards and an analysis of the city's ability to withstand and control those hazards. According to the report, seven types of weather-related hazards may affect the Olympics: rainstorms, high temperatures, hail, high winds, dense fog, thunder and lightning, and haze.[8]

Determined not to let anything spoil the event, organizers of the 2008 Summer Olympics said that they will take control over the most unpredictable element of all: the weather. While China's Olympic athletes were getting ready to compete on the fields, its meteorologists were working on the skies, attempting the difficult feat of making sure it doesn't rain on the August 8th opening ceremonies. "Our team is trained. Our preparations are complete," declared Wang Jianjie, a spokeswoman from the Beijing Meteorological Bureau, addressing a news conference at the headquarters of the Beijing organizing committee in January.

The Chinese are among the world's leaders in what is called "weather modification," but they have more experience creating rain than preventing it. In fact, the techniques are virtually the same. Cloud-seeding is a relatively well-known practice that involves shooting various substances into clouds, such as silver iodide, salts and dry ice, that bring on the formation of larger raindrops, triggering a downpour. But Chinese scientists believe they have perfected a technique that reduces the size of the raindrops, delaying the rain until the clouds move on.

Of course, we are reminded by Scripture that an ordinary man, like Elijah, prayed earnestly that it

8   http://en.beijing2008.cn/news/dynamics/headlines/n214181771.shtml

would not rain, and it did not rain on the land for three and a half years, not just one day! Again when he prayed, the heavens gave rain. (James 5:16) So who is the ultimate weather modifier? Is it not the creator of the universe?

While China was busily preparing for the Olympics, churches from around the world also seemed to be taking this unprecedented opportunity to prepare for outreach during the Olympics. However, there was unhelpful high-level publicity about plans to evangelize at the 2008 Beijing Olympics. Christian mission groups from around the world planned to defy the Chinese ban on foreign missionaries and send thousands of volunteer "evangelists" to the 2008 Beijing Olympics. The level of enthusiasm did not necessarily match the depth of wise understanding. The Chinese tradition gives praise to those who are both *Yong*, 'courageous', and *Zhi*, 'wise'. Zealousness without wisdom often causes backfire.

In the 12 months leading up to the Olympics, the Chinese government launched a massive expulsion campaign of foreign Christians, encoded Typhoon No 5. The campaign is believed by some to be part of the "anti-infiltration" efforts to prevent foreign Christians from engaging in mission activities. Whether this operation is linked with the Beijing Olympics is uncertain. Some of these workers had been serving in China for 15-20 years before they were asked to leave.

This was probably the largest expulsion of foreign workers in the past 20 years.

It is important that we continue to pray for Christian professionals who have been serving in China long-term. Many of these are serving humbly in strategic places, making a significant positive impact on society, those who serve among the disabled, those in medical service, in vocational training for the youth, in teaching business ethnics, in poverty relief work, in AIDS prevention, to name but a few. Pray that they may continue to serve without hindrance. Pray also for the local churches. The spirit of the Olympics will give plenty of opportunities for local churches to reach out to the youth through sports. Pray for creative ways to reach out to the society.

Diaspora Chinese scholars and the Third Church

Statistics from 2005 from China's Ministry of Personnel show that overall barely a quarter of Chinese scholars who have studied abroad returned. By the end of 2005, over 930,000 Chinese scholars had studied abroad with approximately 230,000 returning to China over the last decade.[9] In an effort to attract another 200,000 overseas Chinese scholars to come home in the 2006-2010 period, the Chinese government is making an effort to help these top

1985	125,000
1988	250,000
1989	400,000
1991	640,000
1995	900,000

9   XinHua News Agency January 5 2007.

scholars to lead research in the various fields back in China.[10]

Many top universities in the UK provide scholarships for students from China who will eventually take up major positions of leadership in China.[11] The aim of many of these scholarships is to bring future leaders, decision-makers and opinion formers to the UK for a period of postgraduate study at a formative stage in their careers. Of course, we remember that former Chinese leaders like Deng Xiao Ping and Zhou En Lai studied overseas. According to statistics, around 60,000 Chinese students are in the UK at any one time. Over 52,000 of these students are studying at UK Higher Education level, around 6000 at Further Education level and the rest at Independent schools and colleges.[12]

10   Just in the year 2003, the total number of students and scholars studying abroad is 117,300, among which 3,002 people are state-funded, 5,144 employer-funded and 109,200 self-funded. In the same year, a total number of 20,100 students and scholars returned from overseas studying, among which 2,638 are state funded, 4,292 employer-funded and 13,200 self-funded. As for the geographic distribution of the overseas Chinese students and scholars, the statistics for destination in 2003 is as follows: 10.5% to Asia, 1.8% to Africa, 49.8% to Europe, 15.4% to North America and Latin America, and 22.5% to Oceania. Among those who have returned in 2003, 25.1% are from Asia, 0.2% from Africa, 42.7% from Europe, 22.7% from North America and Latin America, and 9.3% from Oceania. As for those who are still studying abroad, 22% are in Asia, 0.6% in Africa, 28.1% in Europe, 36.4% in North America and Latin America, and 12.9% in Oceania. (from China's Ministry of Education, http://www.moe.edu.cn/english/international_2.htm).

11   Oxford University produced 24 British Prime Minister thus far. The China-Oxford Scholarship Fund China Scholars Newsletter Sept 2005.

12   UK Foreign and Commonwealth Office/ China Scholarship Council: May 2007 Press Release http://www.uk.cn/bj/aboutnew_index.asp?menu_id=337&artid=2454

A mission scholar from OMF coined the term "mahjong theology" to describe the recent phenomena of the Chinese diaspora movement. In response to the developments in quantum mechanics Einstein complained that God does not play dice—the universe's physical functioning is not based on chance. Neither is its missiological functioning. "God is "washing" or shuffling the mahjong tiles," he said. Mahjong is the classic Chinese game similar to a combination of playing cards and dominoes, in which the tiles are shuffled or washed after each game. From this, we derived the term "mahjong theology" to advocate diaspora ministry. In God's sovereignty, God is "washing" the pack, and "shuffling" people from various ethnic groups and cultural backgrounds all over the planet. Just as God "shuffled" Rahab and Ruth into the community of faith at different points in history, so now He is shuffling the Chinese across the world. In Acts 17:26-27 we are told that God made every nation of men, that they should inhabit the whole earth and He determined the times set for them and the exact places where they should live. God did this so that men would seek him and perhaps reach out for him and find him, though he is not far from each one of us." So He still does this today as He did then.

Although it would be difficult to verify, it is estimated that nearly 10% of the Chinese scholars returning to China from the UK have become Christians.[13] One of the greatest challenges for these Christians as they return home is integrating back into the society with a new identity, their identity as followers of Christ. A

13 Paul Pruitt, "Why we must engage in Chinese diaspora ministry?", 2007.

clash of values would become obvious. Many of these "Hai-Gui" need support and encouragement to grow in their faith. Often the "Hai-Gui" do not fit well into the TSPM church or the House Church. Therefore, the phenomena of the "Third Church" has emerged over the years.

The Back to Jerusalem Movement

The BTJ movement is not a recent one. The original idea of taking the gospel "back to Jerusalem" was given to at least five different Chinese Christian groups or individuals during the 1940s. Mark Ma, Simon Zhao and Mecca Zhao were prominent pioneers. In 1942 Mark Ma was called by the Lord to go to Xinjiang to preach the gospel to the Muslims there. The next year the Back to Jerusalem band was formed with the goal of preaching Christ to the outlying areas of China such as Xinjiang and Tibet but also beyond—to the 7 countries of Afghanistan, Iran, Arabia, Iraq, Syria, Turkey and Palestine. Several Chinese Christians got as far as Xinjiang but by 1950 all activity stopped. Some were imprisoned. For nearly 50 years, the vision seemed to have died. But in 1995 Simon Zhao shared with house-church Christians in Henan his vision—and BTJ started up again on an even bigger scale.

In the past few years, the BTJ movement was actively promoted in the West and through a number of significant publications, including the popular book "The Heavenly Man." In 2003, there was the claim that a minimum of 100,000 Chinese missionaries will be trained and sent out over the next few years as a tithe of the house church movement. This vision has generated a lot of excitement among Western churches and even huge donations in supporting this work. However, it is becoming apparent that the view that 100,000 missionaries are being trained for cross-cultural work is far from the real situation.

It is encouraging to note that church networks in several regions, including those in the South West and in the North East have been actively involved in training workers for cross-cultural work. One South-West network has sent out 150 cross-cultural workers to serve among different peoples in China. Churches in one major coastal city are also actively involved in cross-cultural work particularly in the North East among the Chaoxian people. The number of cross-cultural workers being trained throughout China, though unverifiable, is probably in the range of hundreds not thousands. One North East house church network has sent more than 10 workers to Outer Mongolia. Business platforms have also been used as a means of evangelism by some house-churches. While churches in the past have been focusing on training evangelists and church planters, now more churches are aware of the need for equipping believers, particularly the young people, for cross-cultural work. Curriculum are being developed and increasingly training materials are being prepared.

The other major need is the setting up of mission structure. Ralph Winter has claimed that one of the biggest failure of missionaries in the past 200 years is not church planting, but mission planting. The Chinese church will certainly be giving priority to cross-cultural work first to places within China and then in the future to places beyond China. There have been individual examples of missionaries sent out from China to the Middle East in the past few years, but attrition rate has been high because of lack of training and preparation and mission structures. Also, role models are very important. This is an area where God's people from outside China can play a role through sharing of experiences in cross-cultural mission work.

The dilemma continues

Many house church Christians in China still find it difficult to register with the government or to attend the government-organized "Three-Self" church. Some official churches label house-churches as "cults" while others would quietly assist them. The divisions can still be very sharp. Older believers still bear the memory of persecution during the Mao era. However, for many younger believers in both the "Three-Self" churches and the house churches, the antagonism between them seems less intense. A large proportion of the younger generation did not have first hand experience of the persecutions during the Cultural Revolution of the 1960s.

A young believer from Shandong wrote the following to FEBC recently which reflected some of the dilemmas facing those younger believers:

"I was born into a Christian family. I like both the "Three-Self" church and the house-church. Each of these has a different form, resulting from the national religious policy, and has different historical backgrounds. Each has its strengths, and the Lord allows them to co-exist in our country. When the Three-Self church found out my standpoint towards the house-churches, their attitude changed. The church began to reject me. I face attacks from my own church-rumors, gossip, insults and lies. The same situation has happened in the house-church and they have rejected me as being a member of the "Three Self" church."[14]

However, there are signs that new approaches are emerging to tackle the divide between the house church and the TSPM. The Chinese government issued new religious regulations in 2005 which might make it possible for house churches to legally register with the government and not under the umbrella of the TSPM. These new regulations are yet to be tested but certainly bring hope to the situation. The Chinese government may be warming to the idea that Christianity can bring a positive role in building a "harmonious society."

One encouraging development in recent months has been a greater collaboration amongst China's urban house churches. One example was an all-night prayer meeting on New Year's Eve participated by several Beijing urban house church networks. The theme was "Revival for China and in Beijing". Many of these house-church leaders have no political motives and have openly dialogued with the authorities in an attempt to alleviate their concerns.

No one can deny the tremendous growth in the Church in China. There is still a broad controversy regarding the total number of Christians in China today. According to some studies, in 1876, there were

14   FEBC newsletter 2007.

just about 13,000 Protestant Christians and in 1920 the number has grown to 367,000. In 1980 the estimation was that there were about 2 million Christians. By 2007, the official figure revealed a total of 17 million Christians in China. However, the general estimation is that there are about 70-100 million Christians in China today.[15]

Just one example: According to the Religious Affairs Bureau of Jiangsu Province, the number of Christians in the province increased to 900,000 in 1995. In Beijing alone, there is an estimation of about 1 million believers.

The Amity News Service, which is the spokesman of the China Christian Council published the following more conservative figures in January 2008 on the number of Christians in China:[16]

	Number of Christians	Churches/ Meeting Points	Ordained Ministers
Total	18,017,750	32,00 Churches 16,000 meeting points	2,600 (2,000 male, 600 female)

While we rejoice in the numerical growth of the church in China, we need to be aware that this growth is not evenly spread among different people groups in China. The main growth occurs among the Han people in China. Many of the minority people groups including the Tibetans, Ughurs, Kazaks, Zhuangs and Yis, still have very little Christian presence.

15   http://www.ccim.org/node/630
16   Amity News Service, January 24, 2008.

Most of the local fellowship groups are able to meet freely without hindrance in recent years particularly in coastal cities. However, those in minority areas like Xinjiang, Tibet and some remote areas still face strict monitoring and restrictions.

It is estimated that there are approximately 6,000-10,000 fellowship groups in Beijing. Shanghai, one of China's most populated city, has approximately 400,000 believers.[17] Many of these believers in big cities are intellectuals that belong to the emerging middle and upper classes.

It has been encouraging to see the signs not only of numerical growth but also spiritual growth particularly the passion to reach out to the minority peoples. While great animosity occurred in the past between the Han and some of the minority peoples, it is encouraging to know some of the house churches are starting outreach activities among the minority peoples. One particular network organizes short-term teams to bring young people to serve in the North-West during summer. Another group reached out to the Chaoxian people in the North-East. Another group worked among the minorities in the Yunnan province for 1-2 years.

Reaching out to scholars

There also seems to be a growing interest in Christianity among scholars and intellectuals in China. Reports after 1989 showed that as many as 10 percent of students on Chinese college campuses were Christian, but there is no way of verifying this figure

17   Tony Lambert, *China's Christian Millions*, p.268.

independently. One university that actually polled its students anonymously was People's University, in the north of Beijing, normally known as "Ren-Da" in contrast to "Bei-Da", i.e. Beijing University. A survey done in 2001 in Ren-Da, randomly selected, revealed a total of 3.6% of those surveyed admitted they were Christians, and some 60% of the polled group said they were interested in Christianity. Only 5% of those who expressed interest attributed this to contact with a church.[18]

More than half, according to the survey, had acquired that interest through reading, lectures, and elective courses. Overall, many of the students thought it no longer a problem to be known as a Christian on campus. When asked why was there a growing interest in Christianity, the common answer was, "With globalization and post-modernity, we cannot find a clear value system and clear definitions and judgment. In this case, Christianity sets up an absolute value system [for us to think about]."

Some Chinese scholars have taken up a different approach to "Christianity" out of which the term "Cultural Christians" has been coined for a number of years. Many of these "Cultural Christian" scholars show interest in exploring recent Western Christian thought, taking into account China's historical and contemporary cultural context. As one Singapore Chinese scholar put it, "[the aim] is to build a foundation for Christian intellectual cultural space, so that values

---

18   David Aikman, *Jesus in Beijing*, Washington, DC: Regnery Publishing, Inc., 2003.

systems of the "sacred" may have its own cultural capital."[19]

There has been a lot of debate surrounding whether "Cultural Christians" are "Christian believers". Some would have preferred to use the term "MCSC", which means, "mainland Chinese studying Christianity". Certainly, some of these cultural Christians profess faith in Christ. Yet, the majority of them do not identify themselves with any church or denomination and dislike being categorized as "mainstream Protestant" or "evangelical".

It is appropriate to remember Paul's words in 1 Corinthians 9,

> "To the Jews I became like a Jew, to win the Jews. To those under the law I became like one under the law (though I myself am not under the law) so as to win those under the law. To those not having the law I became like one not having the law (though I am not free from God's law but am under Christ's law) so as to win those not having the law. To the weak I became weak, to win the weak. I have become all things to all men so that by all possible means I might save some. I do all this for the sake of the gospel, that I may share in its blessings."

Indeed, we are challenged to become "all things to all men so that by all possible means we might save some," whether our contacts are farmers, peasants, migrants (*min-gong*), scholars or intellectuals.

One of the best national sellers in recent years in China was the book, *A friendly dialogue between an atheist and a Christian*, co-authored by Luis Palau and

19   David Aikman, *Jesus in Beijing*, p.250.

Zhao Qizheng.[20] As many already know, Luis Palau is a reputable evangelist with a global ministry. Zhao is a Chinese scientist, scholar and atheist. *A Friendly Dialogue* is an open and frank exchange on issues of faith, culture, history and politics.

We should continue to pray for Christian scholars who are able to dialogue with other scholars. We are called to love the Lord with all our minds, with all our hearts and strength. Perhaps post-modernity has forced many Christians to de-emphasize the importance of the mind in our faith. Reaching out to Chinese intellectuals and scholars demands our engagement at an intellectual level as a starting point.

The power of urbanization

One of the greatest challenges for churches in China today is the need of the "min-gong", the migrant workers. It is estimated that there are 120 million *min-gong* in China today including some who are Christians. According to the 5th China National Census studies, along with the *min-gong*, the overall number of migrant children reached 19 million.[21] It is also estimated that every year nearly 20 million people in China migrate to cities from villages in rural areas.

What is it that characterizes the *min-gong* in China? Firstly, they have changed their main job from farming to urban work. Secondly, they still belong to the peasant category according to the government records, normally recognized as the lower social class. Thirdly,

20   For more information on the book, see http://www.palau.org/media/press/friendly_dialogue_press_release
21   Nov 2007 "ChurchChina"

normally they are not employers but employees. Often their rights are abused by lucrative employers in urban cities. Fourthly, as they are considered rural people, this people group is often marginalized in the urban cities. Many young people leave rural churches and yet are unable to settle in urban churches because of work demands, cultural shock and other factors. Many rural churches describe their church situation as *huang-liang* meaning "desperate" as only the "old and the weak" remain.[22]

Prior to 1980, church growth in China mainly occurred in the rural areas. However, since 1990, the urban church grew rapidly with the increasing urbanization in China. In 1949, the urban to rural population ratio was 1 to 9 (10.6% to 89.4%). In 1970, it was 1 to 5 (17.4 to 82.6%). In 1980, it was 1 to 4 (19.4 to 80.6%) and since 1985, it was 1 to 2 (36.6 to 76.3%).[23]

Many urban churches are grappling with the issue of how to reach out to these migrant workers. To most, reaching out to the *min-gong* is cross-cultural ministry because of the vast differences in cultural backgrounds and social situations. One of the positive outcomes of the urban migration is increasing partnership between Christian businessmen and churches. Factories in urban settings create job opportunities as well as opportunities to reach out to these young people. Partnerships also seem to develop between rural churches and urban churches. Some of the rural churches are taking proactive steps in sending their own pastors as "missionaries" to cities to reach out to

22   *ibid.*
23   China's Statistical Year Book 1992.

the migrant workers. The opportunity of urban mission becomes tremendous.

Rapid urbanization and globalization have forced many church leaders in China to re-think ministry strategies. For the past 30 years, training of Christian leaders in China has by-and-large been focusing on evangelism, church planting and equipping of the Word. Little has been taught on mission or missiology. However, this scene is changing. More churches are beginning to think seriously of mission. They want to know more about sending structures, how to support missionaries, how to teach mission in Sunday schools etc. The concept of mission is also evolving.

One researcher described the 7 trends of mission ministry in China:

- from rural to urban

- from coastal to the inlands

- from reaching the grass-roots to reaching multiple social class

- from direct evangelism approach to integrative approach

- from receiving to giving

- from within the country to overseas ministry

- from territorialism to partnership

One of the potential contributions of the global church to the church in China is to facilitate indigenous mission movements. It is important to plant churches but it is even more important to plant missions.[24] We need to facilitate what is truly indigenous and yet a biblical movement. The church in China is ready to take the step of faith. It is looking for role models, the integration of the word, deeds and character.

It is also important not to forget the many Christian students in universities in big cities. The early history of the Christian student movement in China is a glorious chapter generally unknown today.[25] The China Inter-Varsity Fellowship was founded in 1945. 168 young students from many universities and colleges met for a historic conference in August 1945 on the hills outside Chongqing. There was a unanimous agreement to form a permanent Christian student organization in China. A constitution was drawn up with a standing committee of 7 students and 7 senior advisors. A monthly bulletin was published. This conference marked the beginning of a revival among students in China.[26] Two years later, this became the largest Christian student movement in the world before it was closed down in the early 1950s.

Waking from the sleep

Napoleon once said, "Let China sleep, for when she wakes, she will shake the world." In recent years,

24   Ralph Winter, who taught and researched in mission for 35 years, made the comment that "the most serious mistake in all of Protestant mission history is the failure of Western missions to create mission structures in the mission field." ("The Challenge for Koreans and Americans Together", a lecture delivered by Ralph Winter, Seoul, November 2005.)

25   This exciting story was chronicled by David Adeney in his book *Chinese Christian Students Face the Revolution* (out of print).

26   Leslie Lyall, *A Passion for the Impossible*, London: Hodder and Stoughton, 1965, p.124.

China has constantly been in the world news. It is also a country with growing economic strength. The label "Made in China" is not to be sneered at any more. Many of the latest IT gadgets including the iPhone are assembled in China. According to various reports, China has the 2nd largest number of billionaires after the United States. The total number of millionaires in China account for 3.3% of the whole population.[27] It is now the world's 3rd largest importer after US and Germany. It is expected to be the world's largest economy if growth continues at its current rate. 33 million Chinese traveled overseas in the year 2007 alone compared to just 30,000 Chinese who travelled overseas at the end of the Cultural Revolution in the 60s.

China has increased its participation in international organizations like the UN, ASEAN, APEC etc, brokered the negotiations in the 6-party talks with North Korea, hosted the Olympics in 2008, the Expo in 2010 and will host many more major events in future. There have also been some encouraging signs in tackling poverty in the country. According to the Asian Development Bank and the UN report recently, 1 in 3 live in poverty in the rural areas in China in 1980 compared to 1 in 10 in 1990.[28] This is a significant improvement.

However, China is also facing some major sociological challenges. First the income gap between urban

27 http://www.chinadaily.com.cn/china/2007-12/31/content_6361786.htm See also http://www.bcg.com/about_bcg/news.jsp
28 Speech by Wen Jiabao, Vice Premier at the opening ceremony of the International Conference on China's Poverty Reduction Strategy, May 2000.

and rural populations has reached a critical level. It has been reported by the Asian Development Bank that China's Gini index, an indicator of income gap, rose from 0.41 in 1993 to 0.47 in 2004.[29] There is also great disparity of income between coastal and inland areas. Shanghai's GDP per capita is about 10 times that of Guizhou, one of the poorest provinces. (56733 RMB versus 5750RMB)[30]

In what he described as an "epoch- making" move, Wen Jiaobao, the Prime Minister, promised 339 billion yuan (more than 33 billion euros) over five years to improve the situation of 800 million peasants, i.e. 66% of China's population, and to curb social unrest.[31] In recent decades, the country's economic development has always focused on the cities; depopulated areas have been much neglected.

The leaders becoming younger

The China Communist Party 17th Congress was held in Beijing in October 2007. President Hu Jin Tao proposed the theory of "Scientific Concepts of Development" which was adopted as an integral part of CCP constitution. Some of the key words in the documents include, "socialist morality, clean economy, people orientated sustainable peaceful development".[32] Hu

29 Normally a Gini coefficient of 0.4 is considered to be an important mark beyond which there is a serious risk of instability for the country. The Gini coefficient is a measure of statistical dispersion most prominently used as a measure of inequality of income distribution or inequality of wealth distribution.

30 National Bureau of Statistics of China.

31 Speech given by Wen Jiaobao at the National People's Congress in June 2006.

32 *China's Daily*, Feb 25, 2008

stressed that it was necessary to scientifically analyze the opportunities and challenges that China was facing in economic globalization, and the scientific concept of development should be implemented in the process of "industrialization, urbanization, marketization and internationalization". His earlier focus on "building a harmonious society" was not included into the constitution. Chinese President Hu Jintao said that the country must earnestly implement the scientific concept of development if it wants to attain various development goals set for the 11th Five-Year Plan period (2006- 2010).[33]

One major change in the Communist Party is the educational background of the party members who have been elevated to the top tier of government. The Party top leaders have been mainly engineers so far. However, it is no longer the case. Of the 10 new members of the Politburo (Politburo Standing Committee), only two are engineers; the rest have diverse backgrounds in economics, management, history and law. The two top leaders, Mr. Xi JinPing and Li Keqiang studied politics and economics respectively. Of the 20 provincial leaders appointed, only 1 was an engineer.[34]

Another significant change is that the new generation of provincial leaders promoted by President Hu is on average five years younger than the existing provisional leadership, and many of them studied economics, management, history and law. Nearly 200,000 officials have been "shifted around" and promotion preference has been given to younger officials with

33 *People's Daily Online*, March 6 2008.
34 Arthur Kroeber, "China Insight: Analysis by Dragonomics Research and Advisory", 25 Oct 2007 No 45.

experience dealing with poverty and rural development issues.[35]

A new social class

There is also a new social class rising in China, of nearly 150 million made up of CEOs of private enterprises, intellectuals who have chosen their own professions, e.g. lawyers, doctors, accountants, managers etc. They represent capital worth of 100 trillion dollars and are 1/3 of China's tax base. The former President began to bring their influential segment into the Chinese Communist Party (CCP) with his "3 Represents" theory, i.e. the development of advanced productive force, orientation of an advanced culture, fundamental interest of the majority of the people. The "Three Represents" campaign is designed to ensure that the communist party extends its membership to private entrepreneurs.

With the rising of a rich middle class and private entrepreneurs in China, we also see a tremendous increase in the number of NGOs is China. It is difficult to estimate the number of local and foreign NGOs in China as there were no official records up to a few years ago. However, some estimate that there could be up to 1 million NGOs including those run by Christians. I was able to visit a nursing home run by local Christians in a mega-city. The need to care for the marginalized and the elderly is recognized. One Christian leader of a church from a coastal city shared with me the "A-F" vision of the church in reaching out to others: A (home for the aging), B (book ministry), C (church min-

35   Arthur Kroeber, "The durable Communist Party", China Economic Quarterly Q1 2007.

istry—discipleship), D (drug rehabilitation), E (Direct Evangelism), and F (Family and marriage counseling). This shows a more integrated approach to ministry.

While churches in the past were more inward looking, churches in China today are actively seeking ways to have a more holistic approach in ministry. Also, there are at least 120 registered Christian book stores in China today. Let us continue to pray for the Christians who can be "salt" and "light" in the society, impacting people and communities around them.

China and beyond—moving away from the centre

The word "China" means the Middle Kingdom. Certainly with the rising economic power, China once again is gaining the world's attention. The study of the Chinese language has become one of the most popular subjects in many universities in the West. Many Christians have high hopes for China, that the Chinese church will play an important role in the world's mission movements. While this paper has been focusing on China so far, it is apt that the title of the paper is "China and Beyond: trends, challenges and mission movements."

Some scholars such as Philip Jenkins and others emphasize a shift of power from Western churches to those south of the equator.[36] In contrast, Professor Andrew Walls, "a historian ahead of his time,"[37] insightfully highlighted the concept of polycentrism: the riches of a hundred places learning from each

36 Philip Jenkins, *The Next Christendom—The Coming of Global Christianity*, Oxford: Oxford University Press, 2002.

37 In *Christianity Today*, February 2007.

other. He believes that there is no one single centre of Christianity or one single centre of missionary activity. He said, "One necessitates the other."

To quote Professor Walls further,

> "But the southern Christian lands do not constitute a new Christendom. Few of them have become homogeneous Christian states. Christian faith is now more diffused than at any previous time in its history; not only in the sense that it is more geographically, ethnically, and culturally widespread than ever before, but in the sense that it is diffused within more communities. It forces revision of concepts, images, attitudes, and methods that arose from the presence of a Christendom that no longer exists."[38]

The best seller in 2005, *The World is Flat* by Thomas Friedman highlighted the power of globalization. "The huge advances in interconnectivity that began in the 90s now allow unprecedented human interaction spanning nationalities, languages and time zones."[39] Globalization has certainly allowed a special window of opportunity for serious partnership in the kingdom business. "Interconnectivity" will become important in the future of missionary movements.

While we rejoice in the growing church movement in China and the strength of the China church, we should not forget the Lord is doing a far greater thing than in China alone.

38 Andrew Walls, "The Old Age of the Missionary Movement" first published in *International Review of Mission* January 1987, pp. 26-32.

39 Thomas Friedman, *The World is Flat*, Farrar, Strauss and Giroux, 2005.

Much study has been done on the Asian Mission-ary Movement. Research by Dr. Bong Ring Ro, a well known Korean missiologist, back in 1990 revealed a growing Asian Missionary Movement. The number of Asian missionaries rose from 1000 in 1972 to 21,000 in 1990. Other reports suggested that Asian missionar-ies reached 67,000 in 2000.[40] Hong Kong sent out 376 missionaries in 2006 with 53% in cross-cultural work.[41] South Korea has sent out a total of 14,000 missionaries serving in 180 countries.[42] Therefore the China mis-sionary movement is only part of God's redemptive plan. Yet we are living in an exciting period of history as we see this plan unfold. We wait prayerfully and expectantly. We also participate and partner with others actively. We are called to serve alongside our Chinese brothers and sisters.

The church in China will continue to grow. Partner-ship with the world-wide church of Christ will be the key to seeing a vibrant missionary movement among different peoples. There is much to learn from the church in China particularly on suffering. Yet the glo-bal church of Jesus Christ also has much to share with the Chinese church: our experience in cross- cultural ministry, mission structures as well as equipping and training of cross-cultural workers. True indigenization is only meaningful when peoples from different tribes,

40   Tan Kang San, A case study of OMF International's involve-ments with Asian Missionary Movements: implications for mobilizing the Asian Church. 2000.

41   Reports from the Hong Kong Association of Christian Mis-sions, 2006.

42   Patrick Johnstone, *Operation World—21st century edition*, Ger-rards Cross: WEC International, 2001. See also Timothy Kiho Park, "Korean Christian World Mission: The Missionary Movement of the Korean Church," Luce Colloqium of Korean Christianity, Nov. 17, 2006.

tongues and nations, are serving together with mutual respect and a common purpose, that is, to be ambassadors for Christ. The potential for China as a sending nation in global mission is tremendous.

Coming full circle

The publishing of a small booklet, "China: Its spiritual Need and Claim", in 1865 marked the beginning of a significant mission movement in China, that is, the vision and commitment to bring the gospel to the inlands of China. Hudson Taylor, having just spent 7 years in China, felt the burden to challenge Christians in the West to pray for China and to bring the good news to the Chinese people particularly those in the inlands. He wrote his booklet with detailed information on the spiritual needs of the Chinese people in the different provinces. No one could imagine the effect that this one man could bring. Lautorette, one of the most reputable historians in church history, commented on Hudson Taylor, "This one man [Hudson Taylor], frail in body and of no unusual intellectual powers, called into being a mission which, consecrated to one great task, the giving of the Faith to all Chinese who had never heard it, was to bear witness to the Gospel in every inland province in China."

Hudson Taylor wrote,

> It is a solemn but truthful thought that our every act in this present life—and our every omission too—has a direct and important bearing both on our own future welfare, and on that of others. In His name, and with earnest prayer for His blessing, this paper is penned:..The writer feels deeply that, as the Lord's steward he is bound bring the

facts contained in this paper before the hearts and consciences of the Lords people. He believes, too, that these facts must produce some fruit in the heart of each Christian reader. The legitimate fruit will undoubtedly be—not vain words of empty sympathy, but—effectual fervent prayer, and strenuous self-denying effort for the salvation of the Chinese....The average population of the at least 7 provinces is 29 million and the average number of Christian workers only 13.

Beloved brothers and sisters, we cannot but believe that the contemplation of the solemn facts we have laid before you has awakened in each one the heart- felt prayer: Lord, what wilt Thou have me to do, that Thy name be hallowed, Thy kingdom come, and Thy will be done in China?[43]

Today, we see a growing thriving church in China. Yet, the work is not finished yet. We pray that there will be an indigenous, mature and vibrant church movement in China reaching out to others, those who are both near and far. Undoubtedly, the facts we have heard today should not result in just vain words of empty sympathy, but rather effectual, fervent prayer and self-denial for His Kingdom. I pray that each will ask the question, "What wilt Thou have me to do, that Thy name be hallowed, Thy kingdom come, and Thy will be done in China?"

Dr Patrick Fung is General Director of OMF International.

---

43   Hudson Taylor, *China: Its Spiritual Needs and Claims*, 1865, p.30.

Asian Mission Movements from South Asian Contexts

Robin Thomson

Cross-cultural mission is part of the DNA of South Asian churches. George Melel arrived in Germany in 1977, sent from India by the Divya Jyothi Mission India, based in Kerala. When he first arrived, people asked him 'Who invited you here as a missionary?' He replied 'Who invited Bartholomew Ziegenbalg or William Carey to come to India as missionaries?' 19 years later, he is still there, working with people of all ethnic backgrounds. Mission happens because you are sent out by the call of the Holy Spirit and the prayer and recognition of the church (Acts 13.1-4).

It's exactly 120 years since the foundation (in 1888) of the Mar Thoma Evangelistic Association, the first mission movement in the modern Indian church. The Indian Missionary society (1903) and the National Missionary Society (1905) were both founded just over 100 years ago, by the same person, Bishop V S Azariah. He was inspired to start the IMS by the missionary vision of Christians in Jaffna, Sri Lanka. In the 1920s Sadhu Sunder Singh is believed to have died while evangelising in Tibet.

The first 50 years of the 20th century focussed on the large scale people movements, the independence struggle and efforts for church union. After the colonial era, and the partition of India, there was a flourishing of Indian missions from the mid 1960s, with groups like the Indian Evangelical Mission, the Friends Missionary Prayer Band, Operation Mobilisation and a number of Pentecostal and independent groups. Today the India Missions Association represents 210 Indian mission organisations, agencies and Church groups and about 40,000 Christian workers within India and beyond.

IMA (Indian Missions Association—founded in 1977) is "the national federation of missions in India, which assists Missions and Churches in the proclamation of the Good news and in making disciples of Jesus Christ among all peoples, languages, and geographical areas through members who partner to share resources, research, and training by their effective accountability and care of their personnel."

Its website (http://www.imaindia.org) has a list as long as your arm of programmes, working groups, structures and issues. It represents the growth, complexity and maturity of the missionary movement in India. And it is only a part of the evangelistic and church planting movements taking place at this time.

Each of the other South Asian countries has its own history of the development of cross- cultural mission, along the same lines as India, though they are less widespread and complex. There is the same mixture of inter-denominational, denominational, local church and individual initiatives. There is also the same progression:

1. *The emphasis on outreach to people within the country,* from the same background and then from different cultural and linguistic backgrounds. St Andrews

Church in Lahore, for example, had the 'St Andrews Sending Fellowship' in the 1970s, bringing together young graduates with a vision for mission, who are now leaders in mission organisations both within Pakistan and outside.

2. *The impulse to follow the diaspora movements to other countries.* In the early 1970s, for example, Vivienne Stacey, a Bible teacher with Interserve in Pakistan, began visiting the Gulf to minister to the Pakistani Diaspora Christians there, with the vision to strengthen their discipleship and equip them for outreach to their host communities.

As South Asians settled in the UK, attempts were made to minister to Christians and reach out to others. Some were initiated by mission agencies—for example Wilfred Paul was invited by Interserve to come from India to work in Bolton, and GI Ebenezer came from India to work with Tamil people, in partnership with Indian Evangelical Mission. Some were members of Christian families who had migrated for work, or came independently, like Pastor Massey, who started the Oxford Asian Christian Fellowship. Others were themselves converts in the UK, like Kuldip Rajo, who worked with Clive Thorne, an ex-OMer, to start the Southampton Asian Christian Outreach (now Lighthouse International Christian Church).

The civil strife in Sri Lanka has sent hundreds of thousands round the world, including Christians who have either been part of the migration or have joined it for ministry. Nepalis have always migrated in large numbers, both to neighbouring countries and beyond. There are said to be over 100,000 in the USA, with the prospect of another 65,000 visas allocated for those displaced from Bhutan. Civil strife continues to be a powerful factor in migration and mission.

3. *Sending missionaries to other countries to reach out to the local population.* This was relatively simple between some South Asian countries, for example India, Nepal and Bhutan, but more difficult or impossible between others, for political reasons.

Going further afield was problematic, primarily for economic reasons, either because it was relatively too expensive, or because of foreign exchange constraints. Tentmaking was one possibility. In the 1990s a few Indian and Pakistani tentmakers were working in some Central Asian countries where business opportunities were available. The other avenue was through partnership with an international organisation. Indian Evangelical Mission had partnership agreements with OMF, Interserve and other organisations to send workers to Fiji, Thailand, Afghanistan and elsewhere.

Opportunities and challenges today

Today, with the explosion of opportunities for professionals, as well as the growing economic prosperity of South Asia, there are South Asians everywhere, and opportunities for mission within any population.

Looking at mission in and from South Asia, there are 3 directions to keep constantly in mind

To South Asia: reaching the unreached there
  Working with churches and missions in South Asia
  Working with diaspora South Asians who are reaching back to their 'home' people

To the diaspora: reaching unreached South Asians there (Hindu, Muslim, Sikh and others)

From South Asia and the Diaspora to the rest of the world

When South Asian Concern began we had a vision called 100/100/100. This stood for 100 new workers to South Asia; 100 new tentmakers working within the countries; 100 going to work in other countries. This was in large part fulfilled—though not in exactly the way we had expected.

The opportunities are unlimited. The challenges are the same as they have always been: economic imbalances, distortions from the colonial period, different styles of leadership and management, cultural differences. In 1993 Dr L.N. Tluanga and I (both working at that time with Interserve India), were asked to write papers on this topic for the 1994 United Conference of Interserve. The issues we listed are all relevant today. Dr Tluanga's suggestions for moving forward are also familiar:

1. The goal must be clear
2. We must do it step by step
3. We must count the cost
4. It is an on-going process
5. We start by evaluating our resources
6. We need to pray together and give together

> What are some of the key tensions—or creative opportunities—in the South Asian context?

Here are a couple of examples:

(a) *Finding the balance* between the corporate organisational structures that have been very effectively used by Western churches and missions (and by others—look at the structures set up by India Missions Association) and the more relational family type structures used by many South Asians.

Many of the South Asian Christian fellowships in the UK have links with North India and Pakistan, where their members originate, and they are keen to use these, both to strengthen the churches and to reach out. So they each have their 'family' mission structure and activity, some with officially registered trust/charity status, others informal. The style is family based and entrepreneurial. For example, a woman who came to the Lord in the UK has given land back in her home village, where there are no Christians, to build a church.

'Mainstream' churches and mission organisations are looking to recruit South Asians to go and work in South Asia, but sometimes find it difficult, even with the younger generation, who have grown up in the more corporate, multi-cultural environment.

Perhaps it is easier to see the need for this when seeking to work in a third culture or country.

(b) The diversity of cultures between South Asian communities. The 'Jewels in His Crown' conference, for example, which brings together ministries among South Asians in the UK, is very much a cross-cultural enterprise, not just between Asian and non-Asian, but between Asians. This also makes corporate activities and partnerships harder, but also, in many ways, more relevant.

How do we respond? This is a re-phrasing of the suggestions made by Dr L.N. Tluanga and discussed in the 1994 conference.

We need to clarify the goal of partnership

Our goal is to work together to reach the unreached. It is not partnership for its own sake. It is not just exchange of personnel, though that is valuable. It is recognising that we can and must work together and share resources in order to be more effective in reaching out. Churches from different cultures, geographical, economic and spiritual backgrounds have different resources to contribute.

George Melel, William Carey, and Bartholomew Ziegenbalg would need to qualify their answer to the question 'who invited you?'. They were sent by the Holy Spirit, but would recognise the importance of relating to the local churches and other Christians, if they existed where they were going. (Ziegenbalg's mission was a classic example of partnership—a German sent by the king of Denmark through an English mission society to India).

We need to confront the obstacles to partnership

These are primarily economic and socio-political, linked to the colonial past and the current unequal structures of our globalised world. In a word, they are linked to power and inequality.

We need to acknowledge and face them with a regained Biblical perspective: one world, created and redeemed by the One God, needing to hear the message of redemption and transformation through his church. Mission is not just from 'here' to 'there'. It is in all directions. This is all the more relevant and possible in our age of large-scale diaspora movements, which have re-written geography and added to the complexity and richness of our task. We all have the privilege and responsibility not only to engage in this ourselves but to encourage, challenge and facilitate each other.

> Authentic partnership is actually between two crippled partners—the blind and the lame—who cannot go on a journey unless the lame person provides eyes for the blind and the blind person provides legs for the lame. Most partnership is not worked out by sitting and talking about it. It is worked out by setting out on the journey.[1]

The apostle Paul showed himself fully aware both of this biblical mandate and the complexities of fulfilling it. We see him going as a pioneer himself, encouraging the new churches to be involved, picking up a multi-cultural team from the new churches, maintaining good communication with the sending churches, recognising economic issues by taking finance where

1   Vinay Samuel and Chris Sugden, quoted by Stanley Davies, 'Can We Work Together?' in *The World Christian*, Nottingham: St John's Extension Studies, 1991, p 89. This is a useful summary of the issues of partnership.

it was needed, and inviting the church in Rome to finance and support his proposed mission to Spain.[2]

We need to commit ourselves to work together for the long haul.

This includes

•   showing mutual respect

•   looking for ways to share, facilitate and make connections

•   giving space and freedom: don't always offer to help or intervene

•   accepting different styles of working and management

•   building multi-cultural leadership

•   talking openly and frequently to each other (use the appropriate style of communication—is it email? phone? letter? face to face meeting? a combination?)

•   recognising that situations are constantly changing and developing, as cultures change

Relationships are the key, as each situation may demand a different approach. And relationships take time and effort for trust to develop.

2   Luis Bush, *Funding Two Thirds World Missions*, Paternoster, 1990 has a sensitive discussion on the potential and pitfalls of money in developing partnerships.

Is it worth going beyond our own structures and cultures to spend the time and effort to understand and work with people of other backgrounds? Don't we have enough to do already? There will be misunderstanding and tensions. We will have to spend time to sort these out. We will have to say "sorry", not once but many times. Is it worth the effort? Why not work separately in our own cultural and social groups?

Robert Warren describes the questions when a new leadership structure was introduced in the growing church of which he was minister:

> "Will this make for twice the strength, or double the hassle? Our early experience would suggest that it will do both." [3]

Partnership will involve us in extra effort, extra cost. But it will double or triple our effectiveness in mission. We need to make conscious attempts to change our thinking and attitudes, our terminology and expectations. If we think it is complex, that is how the world has become today. Our inter-twining relationships can either become bureaucratic and choke us, or they can be rich and creative, enabling us to do what we never expected before.

We all need to rethink and restructure ourselves and our organisations, so that we can enter fully into God's multi-coloured plan.

3   Robert Warren, *In the Crucible*, Highland Books, 1989, p 211.

We live in a world which has become a marketplace of ideas and values. Buddhism, Hinduism, Islam, Marxism, materialism—and many others—compete for the hearts and minds of the whole world. The multinationals have spread the Gospel of Coca Cola to the corners of the planet. Petrodollars have helped to export and establish Islam from West to East—in Regent's Park, Hong Kong or Meenakshipuram. Each of these faiths and ideologies wants to be seen as the universal faith.

We have discovered the truth in Christ, or rather we have been discovered by Him. We know that He is the Way for all people. But for many, Christ is a Western figure, for Westerners; as Buddha, Krishna and others are for their own people. They will acknowledge Him as universal Lord only when they see Him incarnated and brought to them by men and women from all races and cultures.

It is beginning to happen today, on a world-wide scale—a fulfilment of God's plan to demonstrate His "multi-coloured wisdom" to the whole universe through the church (Eph 3.9f). If this means anything it surely means that God intends the gospel not only to be received by people of every colour and race and tribe and language, but also to be carried by them. This will be a demonstration of the universal lordship of Christ.

Appendix: some practical possibilities

Strategic partnerships

These bring together individuals or groups who are seeking to reach a particular place or people. They agree to focus together on evangelism and church planting among that people or in that place, and to share resources for this. This kind of partnership is also described as a "Vertical Partnership". ("Horizontal Partnerships" bring together people in the same speciality—e.g. literature or radio or medical work—spread over a variety of places). These strategic partnerships are very powerful and effective. But they require effort and the will to work together and face the problems of relationships, structures and policy on the ground.

Sharing personnel through secondments, joint projects or exchanges

Kachhwa Transformation Ministries, working in wholistic ministry in a large rural area in North India, is inviting other organisations and churches to join with them to take responsibility for a part of the area. They will share infrastructure, orientation, training and other key resources, but will have freedom to start and care for the churches in their part of the area.

Cross-financing

- A mission in the UK provides finance to a group of missions in India to send missionaries to a third country.

- Using business to generate finance for evangelistic work.

Prayer networking

For example, encouraging prayer conferences for world mission. In the early 1980s Love Maharashtra organised some prayer conferences, in partnership with Interserve and other groups. They helped to give people a broader vision and resulted in sending missionaries. "Adopt-a-People" is a powerful way for a local church to be involved effectively and strategically in world mission—in partnership with others. In India this is called "Serve-a- People". (Details from the India Missions Association). It provides information about unreached groups and about churches, agencies and individuals that are seeking to reach them. A local church or fellowship commits itself to pray specifically for the needs of that group; to find out about the Christian workers there and encourage them; to seek to send workers from their church. They commit themselves to serve the people of that group through prayer, giving, sending or going.

Creative training

Facilitate exchanges of personnel for training. Send missionaries to another country or culture for training. Japanese students came to India in the 1960s in order to prepare for cross-cultural mission in India and other countries. If this is done creatively, it can be a powerful way to facilitate partnership in all directions—the opposite of the usual "brain drain" to more affluent countries.

Build missionary movements, not just churches

Encourage churches to reach out from the earliest possible opportunity. This will naturally follow the stages mentioned in Acts, beginning from home. But be prepared for surprises and willing to "leap-frog" to people of different cultures or further away, if this is appropriate and God's Spirit guides in that way.

Send personnel to another country to be a catalyst for joint mission. For example, the Brazilian Baptist church sent a worker to India to work with Baptist churches there to get involved together in mission to unreached groups.

Develop multi-cultural leadership

There is a definite place for mono-cultural groups with their own leadership. It is much simpler and can be effective. But for cross-cultural ministry there is a lot to be gained by working consciously at multi-cultural leadership. It is a part of our message.

Encourage team ministry

Encourage team ministry—take people with you for evangelism and ministry. This is the most practical way to begin. Consciously ask yourself whom you can involve with you in this way. The Ministry Fund of Interserve could be a source of extra funds to cover expenses for this.

This also needs to be encouraged by mission leadership

- for our own sakes, because this is a Biblical pattern

- as a way of working more effectively.

Try to place people in teams rather than alone.

Encourage them to link up with other workers in the same place. The arrangement can be formalised by secondment, if appropriate. For example, EFICOR workers co-operate closely with other missions in Bihar and Orissa.

Robin Thomson served for many years as a Christian educator and leader in India. He is currently associated with South Asian Concern.

Who is in the Driver's Seat?

A critique of mission partnership models between Western missions and East Asian mission movements

Kang San Tan

The church in East Asia is growing at a phenomenal pace, both in spiritual vitality and missionary enthusiasm. For example, The Korea World Missions Association (KWMA) claimed that there were 14,086 Korean missionaries in 180 countries in 2006 (about 19,000 according to non-official counts).[1]

India and the United States of America represent the two largest contributors to Protestant cross cultural missionaries. The Indian Missions Association represents more than 200 mission agencies working throughout India and beyond.

However, some Western mission groups still operate without much reference to these growing indigenous mission movements from Korea, India, Philippines, Singapore and China. When partnerships are formed, non-Western members are commonly invited to join some elite club to perpetuate the mission goals and boundaries set by existing structures. Unless both parties explore new models of genuine partnership, many of our mission endeavours may lead to

1 Julie Ma, "The growth of Christianity in Asia and its impact on mission," *Encounters Mission Ezine*, 16 (Feb) 2007, pp. 1-7. See Mark Oxbrow and Emma Garrow, *Emerging Mission*, CMS/IEM/ISPCK, 2005.

duplication, wasting of resources, reinventing the wheel, and repeating the past mistakes of colonialism and imperialism. Past Western paternalism still exerts its control due to the fact that the power associated with mission paradigms, leadership patterns, structures, economics and technology is still located in the hands of Western churches and agencies. Lest we think the problem of control and power is primarily a "Western problem", we will see that newer sending mission structures from Asia are also repeating the same mistakes.

The term Asian Mission Movements (AMMs) refers to various Asian churches, mission structures, indigenous mission organizations, and alliances that seek to spread the gospel cross culturally, both within and beyond national boundaries. AMMs do not necessarily comprise a centralised or organised network but consist of many local communities—churches and indigenous groups engaged in cross cultural witness.

In reflecting on the AMMs, there are at least two caveats. First, the danger of Asian ethnocentrism, which claims that this is the Asia Pacific Century, and that leadership in mission belongs to the Asian church. The reality is that Christ's mission is the concern of the whole church from all six continents. The AMMs need the contribution from a broader, international, and missiological community, recognising that there is much that newer missions can learn from "Older Sending Nations".

Second, one needs to be careful of the tendency to generalise Asian missionary movements as a single stream, thus overlooking the unique stages and distinct characteristics of each national missionary movement. The issues faced by the more established Korean, Filipino and Chinese missionary movements may differ greatly from issues faced by the emerging Malaysian, Thai and Japanese movements.

The terms "West" and "Western Mission" refer mainly to mission bodies that share their origins to 19th century Protestant mission from Europe and North America. Although every generalisation can be faulted, I trust there are certain common issues faced, models developed, and concerns which have arisen from the AMMs which we may reflect on together. This article is a critique of Western mission that still operates in the outmoded paradigm of control. It explores possible changes in mission partnerships through case illustrations where national players are given an active rather than peripheral role.

Challenges Facing Asian Mission Movements

The Asian Mission Congress I (AMC I) was held in Seoul, Korea in 1990. One thousand three hundred and two participants from 50 nations gathered in Asia for the first time to consider the challenge of missions. Asian Mission Congress II (AMC II) was held in Pattaya, Thailand with 390 participants from 15 nations who gathered to review and follow up on issues facing Asian mission. David Pickard, a former General Director of OMF International presented a paper on "Challenges Facing Asian Missions" at AMC II, and highlighted a number of issues facing the AMMs.[2] I have built on his listing and added additional challenges:

• The need to mobilise the local church for long term missions

• Lack of role models of effective career missionaries

• Need of more examples of responsible, sending churches

• Inadequate sending structures (candidate screening, missionary preparation, field leadership, member care). In particular, member care is still lacking when compared to the level of care provided by International Missions.

• Lack of Asian missionary trainers

• Lack of community based training centres

• Need to develop creative ways in mission among restricted contexts

• Need for field research on Asian missions (strengths, weaknesses, problems faced etc.)

The above list informs us that there are still "gaps" in the growing Asian mission movements which will respond to meaningful mission partnerships.

Implicitly, the list sets out a case against newer Asian Mission Movements which prefer to do mission without partnering with older sending structures from the West. Nevertheless, if partnership means mission

2 David Pickard, "Challenges facing Asian mission," in Castillo, Met, ed. *World Missions: The Asian Challenge*, Manila: AMC, 1991, pp.41-50.

policies and strategies are formulated predominantly through Western eyes and ears, then the primary participants in such partnerships are going to be limited to AMMs who are willing to share a similar ethos. The vast majority of newer Asian churches may no longer be interested in partnering with Western agencies that "use" Asians as some exotic displays to fulfil their own agendas. It could be said that tokenism can be a far worse mistake than peaceful co-existence in mission partnership. From the perspective of newer Mission movements, will it be better to make mistakes and learn from those mistakes than to buy into certain structures and paradigms of missions whereby inherent weaknesses are imposed externally?

Defining the Partnership Problem:
Who is in the driver's seat?

Partnership is a relationship entered into because of the different strengths the partners have. For example, Western partners may contribute mission expertise and funding resources while the Asian partners contribute local field knowledge, passion and growing missionary force.

However, both parties face the problem of operating with old paradigms of mission thinking. Notably, this happens when Western agencies refuse to give up control, or when Asian churches merely look to Western partners for financial assistance. A core ideal in any effective partnership is the concept of "equality and mutuality". While both Western and Asian partners agree on this biblical and strategic ideal, when it comes to working it out in practice, Western-Asian partnerships are fraught with numerous difficulties. As traditional Western partners and emerging Asian missionary churches are negotiating their respective roles, most partnership models neglect the crucial role and views of a third party: namely the national church and indigenous mission movements.

To simplify our evaluation of this complex problem, we limit our discussion on mission partnership to three parties in mission:

a)   Traditional Western mission agencies (denominational and interdenominational missions)

b)   Newer sending mission agencies from Asia (denominational and interdenominational missions)

c)   Indigenous and national church mission movements. Samuel Escobar describes these movements as "another missionary force" and "missionary from below" that do not appear in mission records drawn up by specialists or theoreticians of missions.[3]

In most countries, we assume that there is now a mature national leadership whose views and counsels must be part of partnership models. Unfortunately, there are still mission models that allow leaders to strategise and make plans outside the contexts of the people and cultures they seek to serve. The indigenous missiological principle argues that good partnership models must promote the self-governing of churches and mission projects in such a manner that ownership and future direction are firmly in the hands of national

3   Samuel Escobar, *A Time for Mission*, Leicester: IVP, 2003, pp. 15-16.

leaderships. Foreign partners must seek to serve the interests of emerging local churches, not their own interests.

Incarnation as a Partnership Model: Some Reflections on Power and Spirituality in the light of Philippians 2:5-11

It is easy to talk about partnership in mission, but why are there so few exemplary models of mission partnerships? More than an issue of strategy, perhaps the answer has to do with how one handles power. This article would like to suggest that promising new models of partnership between established Western agencies and newer emerging mission movements can only be undertaken when all parties are willing to adopt 'Downward Spiral Spirituality'; where each party adopts four basic approaches as they work together:

1.   Issue of *attitude*: "Have this mind among your-selves" (v. 5)

> Thou would perhaps be ashamed to imitate a lowly man; Then at least, imitate the lowly God (St. Augustine)

> For you know the grace of our Lord Jesus Christ, that though He was rich; yet for your sake he became poor, so that by His poverty you might become rich (2 Corinthians 8:9).

For Adam and Eve, the issue was to become like God. Sin entered into the Garden of Eden due to the exist-ence of Satan. For Israel during the First Century in Palestine, the older brother's difficulty in celebrating the younger brother's new found role had to do with the former's self-introspection in finding his place in the family. In the same way today the real issue is not about who is in the driver's seat, rather it is about the *attitudes* of whoever it is that is given that role of driving the mission agenda. New partnership attitudes can lead to sacrificial ways that result in newer mission movements benefiting from the expertise of older mission structures.

2.   Issue of *surrendering rights*: "Who, though He was in the form of God, did not count equality with God a thing to be grasped" (v6)

Equality with God is something which Christ already possessed. Before our Lord was born in the likeness of man, he already pre-existed in the form of eternal Divine Being. The statement does not tell us how Christ *refused* equality with God, or how he achieved equality as a reward, but *how he used it.*

Over against the standard picture of oriental despots who understood their position as something to be used for their own advantage, Jesus understood his position to mean self-negation, the vocation described in vv. 7-8... The pre-existent Son regarded equality with God not as excusing him from the task of redemptive suffering and death, but actually as uniquely qualifying him for that vocation.[4]

As long as Western agencies and foreign Asian partners are unwilling to abandon self-interest and refuse to adopt the incarnational model of Christ, partnership will remain a nice slogan around mission conferences and conceptual papers.

---

4   N.T. Wright, "*harpagmous* and the meaning of Philippians 2:5-11," *Journal of Theological Studies* 37:2 (1986), pp. 321-52.

3. Issue of *identification*: "But emptied himself, taking the form of a servant, being born in the likeness of men" (v.7)

Biblical scholars such as Joachim Jeremias find many echoes of Isaiah 52:13-53:12 in the phrase "taking the form of a Servant;" (Phil 2:7) indeed this may be a direct reference to the Servant of Isaiah 52:12. Peter O'Brien argues that, "it seems best, on balance to understand the expression ('taking on the form of a servant') against the background of slavery in contemporary society." O'Brien argues that slavery pointed to "the extreme deprivations of one's rights; even giving up those rights relating to one's own life and person." [5]

Each partner must come to the table of fellowship on the premise that he or she must give up their rights for the interests of God's kingdom. Identification refocuses each partner's attention to the local communities, rather than the interests of the sending churches or foreign mission partners.

4. Issue of the *crucified life*: "Being found in human form he humbled himself and became obedient unto death, even death on a cross" (v.8)

Paul saw Christ's death on the cross as the ultimate act of self- humiliation, for on the cross Christ took our sin and the wrath of God upon himself. Christ freely chose to become mortal man and became a model for missionaries who are genuinely seeking to walk in the ways of the cross. Therefore, genuine partnership will only work if each party is willing to live out the self-less life of servanthood. Sometimes, the process

5   Peter T. O'Brien, *Commentary on Philippians*, Grand Rapids: Eerdmans, 1991, p. 220.

of working with emerging Asian mission movements stalls because it touches on uncomfortable mission lifestyles and use of money. Foreign mission partners are used to certain ways of doing mission and partnership with local or Asian Christians reveals that there are other models of mission that require sacrifices and living at the economic level of the poor.

Case Illustrations of Partnership Models in Asia

• A significant means of partnership is in the area of *mission training*. Notable Mission Training centres in East Asia are: Global Ministry Training Centre (GMTC) in Korea, the Outreach Training Institute (OTI) in India, and the Asian Cross-Cultural Training Institute (ACTI) in Singapore.[6]

Nevertheless, there is still a lack of cross-cultural mission training centres that offer full time and residential training. Some mission leaders from Asia may even assert, 'We don't need more Western evangelists. Rather, we need more theologians and missionary trainers'. The leadership of these training centres must be under national leadership, but foreign partners can be part of the team, contributing specialties in the areas of missiology, religious studies or historical studies.

• Establishing *indigenous mission organizations* is another needed model in Asia. Western and International mission agencies can assist in establishing indigenous missions in Asia. The danger comes when

6   See Miguel Alvarez, 'Missionary Training: A Discipline,' in JAM 2/1 (2000), pp. 91-102, and David Harley, *Preparing to Serve: Training for cross cultural Mission,* Pasadena: William Carey Library, 1995.

foreign groups, consciously or unconsciously, attempt to produce replicas that may not be suitable for newer missions. Instead, foreign partners need to realize that there are now mature indigenous leaders in each of these countries.

Therefore, partnerships could be formed between foreign partners and the leadership of national Christians in countries such as Thailand, Laos, and Vietnam rather than simply between foreign partners. Field strategies should no longer be determined without adequate input from national leaderships. The Mekong area is an example of a place where hundreds of foreign mission agencies have planted their foreign flags in the region. Why can't these foreign agencies talk to one another, and listen to mature national leaders as to how they can best serve God in Mekong? The question of who is in the driver's seat is a pertinent one!

• Japan is an economically rich nation with fewer than 1% Christian population. There are still many small towns of 200,000 people without a significant Christian presence. The old paradigm is to send foreign missionaries to Japan, with the foreign partners planning field placements and bearing the cost of mission support.

There are now models where local Japanese churches or denominations identify a mission outreach, and then request missionary help to form a structure where there is a nucleus of local believers working under national leadership. A committee of the *inter-church association* is established to oversee the planting of a church in a particular area. The committee provides the finance for a meeting place and the

Japanese evangelist's salary; the non-Japanese mission agency may send foreign mission partners and provide for the salaries of these foreign workers.[7]

• In the Philippines, a few foreign mission agencies have partnered to establish the *Alliance of Bible Christian Communities of the Philippines* (ABCCOP). This partnership has progressed from being a mission initiated and directed organization to a self-governing body. Today, the four expatriate missions relate to one another as partners and serve under the national leadership of ABCCOP. There are regular meetings of the respective directors to coordinate ministry, plan and strategize together. No foreign mission agency makes major field decisions without consultation and interaction to some degree with partners and contributors from the national church leadership.

• The Philippine Missions Association presents a case of partnership of mission bodies at a national level. In a way similar to the practice of the Indian Missions Association, the Philippine Missions Association serves as a valuable resource for "outside" mission bodies.

Although many International and Western based mission agencies are aware of these national mission networks, very few have benefited from close dialogues with them because the International Directors are based overseas and have very little time to develop genuine friendships with these national mission leaders. Instead, we find that the Philippine Missions Asso-

7   See a series of articles on "Church-to-Church Partnership" in James Kraakevik and Dotsey Welliver, *Partners in the Gospel,* Wheaton: Billy Graham Center, 2005, pp. 59-90.

ciations developed strategic partnerships with similar sister associations in Indonesia and Korea.[8]

Who is in the Driver's Seat?

Diffusion of Roles, New Problems and Possibilities

Partnership is not just something we need to give lip service to but must be tested by the fruits of partnership, nurtured in mutual respect and carried through in selfless service for the Lord's work. There is a great danger that Western mission agencies and more established Asian missionary churches from Korea, Hong Kong and Singapore 'adopt' national workers or national churches, seeking to do mission out of position of power, and therefore neglecting the crucial principle of incarnational partnership in missions. Past charges directed against Western missions—exporting foreign ways of Church life—are now rightly directed toward some new mission ventures within Asia. Past criticisms that mission agencies do not genuinely partner with local churches are now seeping into many megachurches from wealthier Asian countries which seek to control mission fields from the home base, where decision makers have no understanding of local cultures, and where the church merely do mission through short term visits. Eventually these newer churches are expected to duplicate foreign Christianity exported from Korea, Singapore or Malaysia—just as they once received foreign models from Britain or America.

Partnership remains a buzzword in mission circles, but we should revisit this issue with courage and critique, and ask the question: who is in the driver's seat?

8   See Met Castillo, "The Philippine Missions Association: A Case Study," in Kraakevik and Welliver, op. cit., pp. 141-150.

Should it be foreign mission bodies from the West? Should it be new growing churches from Asia? Should it not be the indigenous churches locally? Clearly, a theological answer to the question as to who should be in the driver's seat is to look to God on the throne! If He is really on the throne, then strategically, it should *not* be foreign powers firmly setting the agendas of missions. A better scenario would be to encourage national churches to learn to drive, with good support from more experienced drivers.

Ultimately God is the driver and in this new era of mission, we can celebrate mission from all six continents where neither West nor East drives the agendas but a new team of drivers from both East and West, rich and poor, career missionaries and migrant witnesses, creatively chart new directions in mission models. Sometimes we must allow others to drive, and be willing to mix up various roles and rules in order to find new routes and discover new sceneries. For such possibilities, changing drivers, rotating drivers and allowing back seat drivers are all good practices, where diffusion of roles can be a good start and provide new surprises along the way.

Kang San Tan is the former Head of Mission Studies at Redcliffe College and Executive Director for Asia CMS.

Mission Asia: Practical Models in Mission Partnership

Patrick Fung

'Partnership' is a strong New Testament concept, and occurs in a number of contexts. James and John were 'partners' with the sons of Zebedee (Luke 5:10) and Paul can speak of 'partnership in the gospel' in Philippians 1:5. Biblical models of partnership include:

- Paul's partnership with fellow-workers such as Prisca and Aquila (Romans 16:3) or Epaphroditus (Philippians 2:25)
- Partnership with already planted churches (Philippians 1;5, 2 Corinthians 1;7) '...because of our fellowship in the gospel from the first day until now'
- Partnership with sending churches (Acts 13:1-3)
- Partnership in sharing support (Acts 20:34) '...supplied my own needs and the needs of my companions'
- Partnership with the Lord (1 Corinthians 3:9) '...for we are God's fellow-workers'
- Partnership in suffering (2 Corinthians 1:7) '...as you share in our sufferings'.

Luis Bush has defined partnership as 'an association of two or more autonomous bodies who have formed a trusting relationship, and fulfil agreed-upon expectations by sharing complementary strengths and resources, to reach their mutual goal'.[1]

The danger of this definition is that it refers only to a task-based relationship. The Biblical model speaks first and foremost of a oneness in Christ and is both a horizontal and a vertical relationship.

Practical models in mission partnership

The first model we could consider is the China Inland Mission (CIM) later to become the Overseas Missionary Fellowship (OMF). This started as a British mission and became an international mission focussing on China.

We shall also look at current China ministry models: a multi-agency model; house churches/ theological institutions/mission agencies working together; a radio and discipleship ministry; churches in Hong Kong and the Chinese mainland; a house-church missions network; Christian professionals, with both foreign and local workers. So that the focus is not entirely on China partnerships in Cambodia, Thailand and the Philippines are also considered.

A historical perspective

The history of the CIM is instructive. Hudson Taylor returned to England for the sixth time between January 1887 and October 1888 to recruit 100 workers for China. ('It is not great faith you need, but faith in a great God...God's work done in God's way will never

1   L. Bush & L. Lutz, *Partnering in Ministry: The Direction of World Evangelism,* Downers Grove, Il.: Inter-Varsity Press, 1990, p. 46.

lack God's supply'—May 26, 1887). A young Princeton graduate by the name of Frost sailed to England to request consideration of his application to join the CIM. His application was refused but he invited Hudson Taylor to the US in July 1888. Hudson Taylor preached at D. L. Moody's Northfield student conference and at Niagara-on-the-Lake. Funds for eight missionaries were received and on September 25, 1888, 14 new workers known as 'the American Lammermuir Party' left Toronto for China with Hudson Taylor. In 1889, the North America Council was established in Toronto. A partnership had been started.

In due course there were many of these. Partnerships were formed with the Bible Christian Mission of England, the Swedish Mission in China of Stockholm (1887), the German China Alliance (1890), the Swedish Holiness Union (1890), the Scandinavian Alliance Mission (1890), the Finnish Free Church (1891), the Swedish Alliance Mission (1892). Also 12 men and women went to China with Hudson Taylor from Australia in 1890. The part played by the Scandinavian Alliance Mission is equally instructive. Their stated aim was to:

> to concentrate on the evangelisation of China within three years, under Hudson Taylor's leadership while responsible to the church sending them...

In the year 1891, 35 left for China on January 17 and a further 15 on January 29. Twelve left for China on February 14, 1892.

What lessons can be learned from this partnership model? Firstly there was a commonly owned vision i.e. reaching China's millions. Secondly there was an understood term, the "Forward Movement" (which asked the "what next?" question) and a correspond-ing attempt to explore synergy. Then there was the importance of communication. The danger of moving too quickly without the understanding of those on the ground was understood. The importance of training was also agreed—many from the associate missions were poorly equipped and prepared, and this had to be dealt with. Finally there was an ownership of goals. The initial goal of recruiting 1000 missionaries took some time to reach, but people were prepared to work steadily to achieve it.

Some current partnership models

1. "SERVE"

"Serve" is an example of a multi-agency model. It is a legal entity, registered as a charitable foundation in Hong Kong in 1987. It is not specifically a religious organization, but is known to recruit Christians. In fact it is a partnership of 13 agencies, a multi-cultural and multi-agency fellowship and a family, united by the vision for Christ and for China.

From SERVE's vision and mission statement clear goals have been agreed.

- Sending Christian professionals into China
- Focusing on the inland—Central and Western
- Emphasising on Christian values
- Word based
- Establishing churches
- A mission movement

"Serve" also has a clear process by means of which partnership is built. It is recognised that time is needed together to work through the details of the common vision and mission at different stages of development. There needs to be an external facilitator. Prayer and sharing are vital so that there can be a building of trust and understanding. Members must be consulted and it is important to ask the what NOT question!

Of course there have been and are challenges. In a multi-agency organisation there are bound to be different agendas. Foreign agencies often lack a full understanding of China. Smaller agencies may feel marginalised and it takes commitment when funding projects together.

Finally "Serve" believes that it has an important next step to take and that is partnership with local Christians and not just other mission agencies.

2.   Agape Project

This was essentially a partnership between theological institutions (outside China), a mission agency and the house church network. The vision (which now dates back to the late 80s) was to equip house church leaders to be solidly based in the Word, effective in church organisation and have a passion for mission. The strategy was based on itinerant training. The leaders of the partnership—from the mission agency, the church network and from two seminaries in Asia (Chinese) developed a four-year M.Div-level programme, with 30-40 trainees who met quarterly for two weeks. So far about 250 pastors have been trained and some of these have been selected for further training overseas. The project has placed great emphasis on the indigenous principle. Thus:

- House church leaders decide on the selection of trainees
- House church leaders are involved in setting the curriculum
- There is an understood role change for trainers—from trainer to facilitator
- Building trust through long term commitment is a priority
- The long term goal is to hand over leadership to house church leaders

3. "Love China" radio ministry

This has been operating for over 40 years. In the past it was mainly directed to rural areas. It has always been strong in evangelism, but has also developed an "On-The-Air" Seminary. 495,000 letters have been received so far, and every year over 20,000 letters come from China.

Why is there a need for partnership? Partnership enables the ministry to identify some key trends and needs, and to respond to them. Here are some of them:

- The rise of the Urban Church
- Church engagement with social issues: e.g. rising divorce rate, integrity, marginalised groups (*min-gong*)
- Church leadership training needs more face to face interaction
- Counseling: a counseling service in partnership with Christian professional counselors and a counseling hotline

- Strengthening and equipping, including pastoral visits to graduates of the "On-The-Air Seminary" by a sister organization
- Publishing, especially providing books/resource materials for church leaders

4. Hong Kong/Mainland Church model of partnership

There is a Biblical model here, the partnership between the church in Antioch and the church in Jerusalem.

There is also a window of opportunity. Ease of travel, available resources, acceptance by the Three Self Patriotic Movement, and the fact that there are 1300 churches in Hong Kong, more than 70% of which are prepared to be involved all contribute to opening this window. Of course there are also challenges.

5. Partnering with Christian Professionals

An example of this would be "To China With Love". The main purpose is the mobilising of Christian Professionals from overseas. These would come at the invitation of the government and serve among some of the minority peoples. They would address key projects that affect the community to do with such fields as livestock, agriculture, medical services and youth vocational training. The next step is to mobilise Christian professionals from within China. The whole idea of Christian professionals as mission partners tends to raise up questions of esteem. Do we consider one another as equal partners? What does that mean: to be equal partners?

1.   OMF Thailand

Here we can discern three levels of partnership:

Level 1 Partnership: fully integrated into the field structure and ministry, based on shared vision, values and commitment

Level 2 Partnership: shared vision and values, but without commitment to share resources or personnel

Level 3 Partnership: assistance in providing visas, but not part of the ministry

2.   OMF Cambodia

The FW publishing house provides another model of partnership. This is an independent not- for-profit organisation, involving a collaboration between churches, Bible colleges and mission organisations. The goal is to publish books by indigenous Christian writers relevant to the needs of church and society. The ministry has produced a number of useful 'lessons'.

•   Ongoing partnership provides the opportunity to review together the original goal of the partnership and adjust appropriately. In this case there was more translation work in the beginning and this was too narrow a focus.
•   Continuity is needed when leadership changes.
•   It is a better situation when each partner provides the initial funds as well as the missionary personnel to make the ministry happen.

3. "Alliance" Partnership in the Philippines

Started 30 years ago by 4 mission agencies, it focused on training of leaders for missions. It has faced a number of challenges:

• Both focus and structure have gone through stages of change
• Nationalistic sentiment sometimes hinders the work
• Some nationals look too much to expatriate organisations for finance
• Wisdom is still needed to know when to pass on leadership to nationals
• Partner organizations occasionally launch out into new ministries without the others' knowledge

Partnership Issues and Challenges in Asian Mission

What are the key issues and challenges that emerge from this review of partnership models? A number of questions arise:

• Will western agencies and missionaries recognize emerging Asian leaders as equal partners and allow them to take on leadership responsibilities?
• Will western agencies be willing to adjust and reorganize their basic structures to be relevant to contemporary Asia and to facilitate the changing roles?

• Can Asian Christian leaders overcome their inferiority complex and avoid a reactionary attitude and pride?

• Will Asian church leaders and missionaries be willing to humbly acknowledge with gratitude the contribution from Western missionaries?

• Can Asian leaders prove themselves to be accountable if funds and resources are entrusted to them?

• Is there a trend moving towards inter-dependence rather than independence?[2]

What are some of the key factors that hinder and promote effective partnership?

By way of summary it would be good to mention some key factors in partnership both on the negative and positive side. These are drawn from a survey of mission partnership in OMF fields. First of all the hindrances:

• Very little time taken to listen to God's leading
• Different core and secondary beliefs and values
• Vision not clear
• Unspoken values not shared by all in partnership
• Powerful but often unspoken reasons for partnership
• Weak infra-structure
• Too little time to develop relationship
• Low level of ownership
• Little communication
• Failure to review partnership and make adjustment

2   Chin do Kham, *Journal of Asian Mission* (2003), pp. 175-190.

Then, by way of contrast the factors that help partnership to prosper:

- Sensitivity to God's leading
- Same core beliefs as well as important secondary ones
- Mutual benefit from partnership
- Clear structure that will accomplish the mission
- Relationship of trust
- High level of ownership
- Clear communication. Nothing is assumed
- Regular review of partnership and willingness to make adjustment

A final thought: there are many 'partnerships' envisaged in Scripture but one which is mentioned perhaps more than any other is the partnership in suffering!

Dr Patrick Fung is General Director of OMF International.

A Critical Appraisal of Korean Missionary Work

Challenges for Western and Global South missionaries[1]

Julie Ma

When we read the Bible through the eye of mission, it soon becomes evident that God established his mission in a unique way. The fundamental element of mission was accomplished by God himself through the death of his Son Jesus on the cross. Thus, the author of mission is God and the history and the entire world are the theatre of his mission, where he selects actors and sets the whole plot. But this mission was to be wrought jointly by God and his people, so God raised up various Christian communities of men and women to fulfil his mission. It has flourished over two millennia through the work of the Holy Spirit.

We can safely say that the Lord of mission has used, in particular, the western church in the last millennium. If western missionaries had not come to our land to share the precious Word of God, there is little likelihood that any of us would have heard the good news of God's salvation message. Therefore, I want to

1   This is an updated version of the paper given at the confernece; the present chapter is a reprint of Julie C. Ma, 'A Critical Appraisal of Korean Missionary Work', in S. Hun Kim and Wonsuk Ma (eds.), *Korean Diaspora and Christian Mission*, Oxford: Regnum Books, 2011, pp. 131-145, and appears here by permission of Regnum Books.

acknowledge the critical missionary contribution of the western church not only to Korea, but to other Asian countries.

It is observed that in the last quarter of the century, God has granted his spiritual and physical blessings in a great measure upon the Korean church. It is also encouraging to observe that Korean Christians have received them with missionary consciousness. Since the late 1970s, the Korean missionary movement has grown rapidly. After a generation, Korean leaders of the church and mission communities began to reflect on various aspects of the Korean missionary movement with critical eyes. In this study, I plan to outline the scope of the Korean mission movement, study key features of Korean missionaries' engagement and evaluate their strengths and weaknesses. I will keep my eyes open to the western missionary movement for any mutual benefits to be learned.

Korean Mission Today

An annual report of the Korean World Mission Association (KWMA) reveals that in 2008, 58 denominations and 217 mission organizations sent 19,413 missionaries to 168 countries.[2] Each year of the previous four years, about 2,000 new missionaries were added. Thus, if this trend continues, by 2030, the total number of Korean missionaries is expected to reach the 100,000 mark. These statistics put the Korean church as the second largest missionary-sending church in the world. It is also revealed that the highest concentration of Korean missionaries is in Asia with close to 12,000 (or 56.2%).

2   Kang Sungsam, "Basic Missionary Training: Bible and Disciple," *Korean Mission Quarterly*, 8:29, 2009, pp. 29-40.

Within Asia, Northeast Asia (5,353) and Southeast Asia (5,337) receive the most missionaries.[3]

In the rapid expansion of the Korean mission force, questions have been raised as to whether their effectiveness corresponds to quantitative growth. There are many positive and creative cases of mission engagement by Korean missionaries, but also an equally good number of cases with cause for concern. Naturally, questions have been raised in the areas of missionary motivation, missiological orientation, cultural adaptability and sensitivity, and so on.

Distribution of Korean Missionaries[4]

Continent	Area	Number of countries	Number of Korean Missionaries	Percentage
Asia	South Asia	4	1,069	5.2%
	Northeast Asia	7	5,353	26.1%
	Southeast Asia	11	3.377	16.5%
	Central Asia	10	1,730	8.4%
	Sub-total	32	11,529	56.2%
Europe	Western Europe	20	992	4.8%
	Eastern Europe	23	996	4.9%
	Sub-total	43	1,988	9.7%

3   *ibid.*
4   *ibid.*

America	Latin America	17	807	3.9%
	North America	6	2,317	11.3%
	Sub-total	23	3,124	15.2%
Africa/ Middle East	East-South Africa	20	823	4.0%
	West-Central	21	355	1.7%
	North African/ Middle East	18	729	3.6%
	Sub-total	59	1,907	9.3%
Oceania	South-Oceania	11	713	3.5%
	Sub-total	11	713	3.5%
Others	Itinerant Missionary		140	0.7%
	Under Care & Furlough		279	1.4%
	HQ Staff		823	
	Sub-total		1,242	6.1%
Total		168	20,503	100%

Key Features of Missionary Engagement
of Korean Missionaries

Evangelism and Church Planting

According to statistics 53.3% of Korean missionaries
(or 6,589) are involved in church planting. Presently,
there are 6,585 churches in existence due to the efforts
of Korean missionaries. Church planting naturally

includes evangelism and thus contributes significantly to the winning of souls.

This is not to deny the importance of church planting; it is not only the preferred work among Korean missionaries, but also Western missionaries according to historical reports. I have seen quite a number of non-Korean missionaries, including Asian missionaries, who are passionately involved in planting church(es). In fact, prior to coming to England, one of our primary works was establishing churches in the northern Luzon in the Philippines, in addition to leadership development and teaching in a graduate school. We witnessed encouraging effects through this work. Below is a little piece of my article regarding church planting that reflects much of our own experiences.

> "They laid rather a heavy emphasis on church planting. For various reasons, a church dedication becomes an important opportunity to encourage the local congregation to replicate the efforts. In this special and joyous occasion, the service rightly consists of lively praises, thanksgiving and a long chain of testimonies. However, in the midst of this celebration, we make it a regular habit to challenge the church to open daughter churches in neighbouring communities. In fact, our covenant with the congregation is that only through the reproducing work, will our partnership continue. This is our commitment to assist or work with them in developing new churches. Such a covenant frequently serves to motivate them to start a new house church in a nearby village where there is no established Bible-believing church. In

fact, some churches, expecting our strong emphasis on reproduction, have already started new works before their church building is dedicated."[5]

However, this mission priority is not without problems. A heavy emphasis on this ministry, both among sending churches and organizations, as well as missionaries, may be in part driven by a too-narrow focus on the theology of the church. First, considering the highly local-congregation oriented ecclesiology of Korean Christianity, this may be in viewed as an aspect of 'church growth' of the sending church. In many cases, church planting is carried out in communities where there have been viable congregations. Sadly, we also witnessed some rural churches in the Philippines, named after the missionary-sending church, where the Korean name is completely meaningless to the congregation. Second, it is also possible that church planting produces a visible sign of a church's missionary accomplishment. Often church dedications become a celebration for the visitors from the sponsoring church, rather than for the congregation. Such an emphasis further reinforces the building-oriented ecclesiology of many Korean Christians

Theological Education

Many are involved in training national leaders in Bible colleges or seminaries, often by establishing new schools; only a small number is assumed to work with existing schools. Some of them undertake fur-

5   Julie Ma, 'Church Planting: Pentecostal Strategy for Mission', in Kay Fountain (ed), *Reflections on Developing Asian Pentecostal Leaders: Essays in Honor of Harold Kohl,* Baguio, Philippines: APTS Press, 2004, pp. 323-55.

ther studies to qualify themselves for such ministries. This is one of the mission patterns that early Western missionaries did quite successfully in Korea, both in general education and ministry formation. Current reports note that about 1,415 missionaries from 867 denominations, that is 11.5% of the total missionary force, are involved in this ministry. This is an indication of a generally agreed notion that a good supply of qualified workers is essential in missionary work.[6]

A focus on theological education[7] is not restricted to Korean missionaries, as the presence of numerous Bible schools in mission fields proves. As understood, theological training is closely linked to the emphasis on church planting. Also increasing are schools for general education. In many places where quality primary and secondary education is not readily available, this is an important contribution to society and, often, although not intended as the primary goal, such ministry contributes to evangelism and church planting.

Some schools established by Korean missionaries have attained recognition by established theological associations, but the majority remain struggling to survive. Their effectiveness is often questioned, especially where there had been other similar schools in

6 Kang, *op. cit.*
7 See 'Theme Three: Mission and Postmodernities', in Daryl Balia and Kirsteen Kim (eds), *Edinburgh 2010: Witnessing to Christ Today*, Oxford: Regnum, 2010, p. 80. It notes, 'the radical change in the way of thinking and of looking at life represented by postmodernity cannot but influence theological reflection and education. The key question for churches to answer may not be so much 'where can I find a graceful God', but rather 'where do I find an authentic spirituality'? To address this need, it appears that theological education should be conversational rather than authoritarian, focusing more on encouraging students to reflect on their own experiences...'.

operation. Lack of cooperation is a significant problem as some schools are staffed mainly by Korean missionaries even after decades of operation. Running a school requires a lot of detailed works for administration, staff management and financial security. This work necessitates careful guidance from professional educators and administrators to prevent any hazards.

Social Work

Social work has been relatively less popular among Korean missionaries in the past, but recently has become receptive. Perhaps this is due to a change in mission trends and its influence upon them. Moreover, it is out of necessity in order to meet the immediate felt needs of people who suffer from hunger and sickness. There are 703 Korean missionaries who are involved in social ministries. This number amounts to 5.3% of the total missionaries. The urgent needs cause them to build hospitals, clinics, orphanages, children care centres and retirement homes. Community service also expands to HIV-AIDS ministry, skills training and agricultural development. I have seen dentists and doctors among short term mission groups who voluntarily offer their services.

In fact, western missionaries were enthusiastically involved in social works. A case in point is William Carey's work with the Indian government on critical social problems, like stopping the burning of widows on the funeral pyre of their husbands. Another example is drawn from Hudson Taylor, who, being a medical doctor, attempted to seek to do what he could to lessen the suffering of people. Through his influence China

Inland Mission founded twelve hospitals within the first fifty years of mission work in China.

Other Ministries

There are 1) discipleship (1,845 people, 14,9%), 2) Bible translation (144 people, 1,4%), 3) literature (139 people, 1.1%), 4) ministry for missionary children (104 people, 0.8%), 5) ministry for foreign workers (83 people, 0.7%), 6) broadcasting work (41 people, 0.3%), 7) children ministry and other works (652 people, 5.2%). This also includes those who are in the preparation process for missionary deployment (52 people, 0.4%).[8]

Staff of Mission Agencies

There are 343 or 2.9% who are working in mission agencies. As staff of missionary sending bodies, their contribution to the mission movement is essential, while their accumulated experience becomes an important asset. The number of other staff members working together are 1,296. Ministries include publication (96 people, 7.4%), continuing education (55 people, 4.2%), communication with missionaries (80 people, 6.2%), mission administration (229 people, 17.7%), missionary training program (296 people, 22.8%), handling mission finance (106 people, 8.2%) and others (434 people, 33.5%).[9]

Mission Works	Number of Missionaries	Percentage
Church planting	6,589	53.3%

8 Kang, *op. cit.*
9 *ibid.*

Discipleship	1,845	14.9%
Education	1,415	11.5%
Social Work	703	5.6%
Medical Service	248	2.0%
Translation	144	1.1%
Ministry for MK	104	0.8%
Publication	139	1.1%
Visitation	52	0.4%
Broadcasting	41	0.3%
Ministry for Foreign Workers	83	0.7%
Others	652	5.2%
Headquarters Staff	343	2.7%
Total	12,358	100%

Evaluation: Strengths

Building relationship with nationals

A relationship between Korean missionaries and local people is surprisingly well-developed, according to research work by Sangchul Moon.[10] This indicates that they consider building good relationships important as partners in God's Kingdom. In fact, this is the foundation for every aspect of mission works because local church leaders are essential co-workers and they have to work together. However, some unfortunately have experienced broken relationships and have internally suffered for many years.

---

10   Lee Moonjang, "Change of Mission Paradigm," *Issues of Korean Mission in the 21st Century: Sulrak Forum*, 1-4 Nov. 2005, pp.14-31.

They are eager to learn local languages even if the level of proficiency may not be adequate. Often it is neither conversationally satisfactory, nor up to the level of preaching and evangelizing. However, there are a handful of missionaries who speak local languages almost perfectly. On the other hand, quite a few of them tend to lay back and never get passionate about achieving these critical skills.[11]

Keeping a good contact with the sending body

Maintaining good communication with the sending church or mission agency is one of their strengths. There is a sense of flexibility against a sense of bureaucracy that is often felt from some western mission organizations. At the same time, this may also indicate instability and lack of organizational strength among many mission organizations and denominational mission boards in Korea. This is attested by the fact that quite a number of missionaries have not secured an adequate level of financial and administrative support from their sending bodies, and it is all left to individual missionaries to maintain a direct contact with supporting congregations and individual donors. (This may explain why missionaries are diligent in communication.)

11   See Stephen A. Grunlan and Marvin K. Mayers, *Cultural Anthropology*, Grand Rapids, MI: Zondervan, 1988, p. 90. It notes that language serves the social group by providing a vital avenue of communication among the members, establishing and perpetuating such institutions. Communication is far more than simple language usage.

Cultural adaptation

Those who come from a mono-cultural setting like Korea find it difficult to adapt and adjust to a new culture. One can conjecture that their firm commitment to mission enables them to overcome cultural differences and daily challenges. In fact, without going through this process of enculturation, one cannot adequately accomplish God's mission because mission is always performed in the context of a culture. It does not mean that all Korean missionaries have successfully adapted to the recipient culture. It is expected that many have made countless innocent and unintentional mistakes. It is also true that, in spite of enculturated behaviours to the host culture, a deep sense of cultural superiority still remains to the home culture.

Spiritual life and prayer

Many of them are firmly committed to prayer,[12] as a hallmark of Korean Christian spirituality. Conceivably this is one of their strengths and a critical element in their missionary achievement. This emphasis is seen both in private and church life. Some missionaries even dare to enter a long-term fasting prayer, for as long

12   11 See Stephen B. Bevans & Roger P. Schroeder, *Constants in Context: A Theology of Mission for Today*, Maryknoll, NY: Orbis, 2006, p. 367 on 'Mission as Prophetic Dialogue': '...the life of prayer of anyone can be a truly missionary act, whether a lay person fully engaged in a profession, an ordained minister or religious involved in pastoral or teaching ministry of whatever kind, a retired person with some leisure, or a person suffering or recuperating from an illness.... Prayer of those engaged in the church's work of crossing boundaries, for peoples struggling with injustice and poverty, for fragile communities of faith, for victims of human-caused or natural disasters—this is a valid way of being caught up in the saving and redeeming mission of God in the world'.

as forty days, which in some cases results in a critical health condition. This influences local churches to commit themselves to prayer more seriously. Most congregations established by Korean missionaries have a substantial proportion dedicated to prayer, such as daily dawn prayer meetings and the like. I have seen one mega church in the Philippines which established a Prayer Mountain, and its daily program includes prayer and fasting, as well as Bible studies and worship in morning and evening. This is almost identical to the way Korean Prayer Mountains do.

Spirituality

Korea's primary religions are Buddhism and Confucianism. However, the underlying religious force for all has been Shamanism, a Northeast Asian form of animism. History reveals that along the way, they were mixed with practices and beliefs of Shamanism and animism. Such religious background explains the unique spiritual orientation of Korean Christianity. Everyone begins with a keen consciousness of the spiritual world, and this contributes to the spiritual dynamic of Korean Christianity. This also significantly helps Korean missionaries to more effectively engage in the various spiritual issues of people in the mission field.

Weaknesses

Missionary motivation

Supposedly, a missionary's firm sense of calling[13] and commitment to mission is his/her foundation for missionary life and work. Indeed, there are missionaries who are deeply dedicated to giving their life to the people they have adopted as their own. On the other hand, mission provides a context where daily ministry demands are significantly reduced in comparison with the Korean setting. The daily routine of an average pastor in Korea begins with an early morning prayer, numerous house visitations, sermon preparation, and others. Many missionaries find their missionary life filled with sudden 'freedom' and some have abused this, as well as the absence of a supervisory monitoring system. This in turn affects their ministries and their relationships with national partners. When a missionary fails to be a model Christian, it is difficult to persuade others to follow Jesus. This leads one to question the very motive of their missionary life. Although a call is private in nature, it is important for mission agencies to develop a process to ascertain one's genuine missionary calling.

---

13   See Julie Ma, *When the Spirit Meets the Spirits: Pentecostal Ministry among the Kankana-ey Tribe in the Philippines*, Frankfurt: Peter Lang, 2000, pp. 74-75. It notes, 'The speaker invited church members who wanted to give their lives for the lost. Her heart was broken as she sensed the presence of God. Vanderbout was one of the first to answer. She almost ran to the altar, put her hands up in a gesture of total surrender and prayed, 'I give myself to You! I will do what You ask me to do! I will go where You ask me to go! Oh God'.

Normally those who come from a monolithic culture tend to view and evaluate other cultures through the standard of their own. This immediately causes some missionaries to push their values, practices and lifestyle on to the host culture. Although there is a fine line between adopting certain positive elements of the home culture and blindly insisting on it, many congregations established by Korean missionaries have adopted some elements of Korean worship[14]. For instance, some churches use a portable bell on the pulpit to signal the beginning of a worship time. Even Korean Christians do not know where it began, and yet such a practice has been uncritically 'imported' into their mission setting.

However, a more serious challenge is the grave difficulty for the average Korean missionaries to break out of their cultural shell and get over the comfort zone of their own culture. This is clearly seen in the common practice of Korean missionaries in associating with fellow Korean missionaries regardless of their denominational orientations, while their interaction with other nationals is far less, even if they are from the same denominational tradition. A tendency is that the more they get together, the more they want to be just among themselves. Such close relationship among themselves frequently causes conflicts, comparisons,

14   13 See Charles H. Kraft, *Anthropology for Christian Witness*, Maryknoll, NY: Orbis, 1996, pp. 70-71. It notes, 'Such condemnation stems from the monocultural habit of *always evaluating other people's customs and perspectives in terms of one's own culturally learned assumptions and values (worldview)*'.

and competitions, thus, creating another form of cultural 'missionary compound.'

Moral laxity

Moral laxity is not a unique problem among Korean missionaries. Lack of a close organizational monitoring system may contribute to this, while a new social and cultural context may make missionaries more vulnerable to temptations. Moral laxity ranges from ministerial attitudes and financial accountability to sexual issues.

This is particularly relevant to Korean missionaries as their traditional ethics is guided by who sees you rather than what you do. This 'face' (or 'shame') cultural orientation can 'release' some from cultural 'restrictions' and give courage for them to behave laxly. And the 'shame' culture further worsens the situation when an incident occurs, as there is a strong tendency to cover up or quietly resolve the problem, instead of correcting the real issue. This is what a concerned observer of Korean missionaries sternly warned:

> This [sexual incidents among Korean missionaries] is seldom discussed openly among Koreans. The result can be immense ignorance and naivety remaining as well as immorality. Some who come to Europe perceive 'the West' as a playground of immorality and a few have indulged themselves. Not reading social signs accurately has led to immense discomfort among western women missionaries who have received unwanted attention

from Korean men on the team. In some cases this
has led to actual sexual assault.[15]

It may be true more among short-term missionaries than long-term ones, nonetheless the observation
is alarming, if it is true. This definitely requires all
Korean missionaries to be culturally and personally
sensitive. Further, this calls for a system of accountability both from the sending body and the closely
knitted Korean missionary communities. However,
more fundamentally, a good dose of cultural learning
should be a part of missionary orientation.

Aggressiveness

Koreans in general are focused and dedicated workers. This explains the economic feat of the country in
less than a generation from the rubbles of the Korean
War. Their movement is swift and decision-making
is often impulsive. Positively, some attribute Korean
leadership in the IT industry to this instinct. However,
such aggressive behaviour, particularly coupled with
poor language and communication skills, can produce
gravely negative effects. National partners can per-
ceive Korean missionaries as domineering, insensitive,
and even 'imperialistic.' It is with mixed emotion that
I heard a comment, "The first words that national co-
workers learn from Koreans are *ppali ppali* or 'quick,
quick'." This, no doubt, contributes to impressive
missionary achievements in many places; however,
this has strong potential to undermine long-term
effects of missionary work, relationships with national

15   Howard Norrish, "An Evaluation of the Performance of Korean
Missionaries," *Issues of Korean Mission in the 21st Century: Sulrak Forum*,
1-4 Nov. 2005, pp. 132-151.

leadership, and more seriously, obsession to visible accomplishments as the goal of ministry.

The Next Step Forward

Having discussed various spiritual, cultural and contemporary resources as well as shady areas of Korean missionaries, how can their experiences also be a resource for other emerging missionary churches in the global South, as well as the old (that is, western) missionary churches? And also what can the Korean missionary movement learn from the long experiences of the western churches and appropriate their resources? Then, how does the Korean experience form the shaping of our own missiology? Some are listed below.

Lessons to Learn and to Be Learned

Commitment and hard work

Although there are a good number of less-than-qualified Korean missionaries who may cause more problems than establishing a viable mission work, it is true that another good number are committed and dedicated to God's work, bearing marvelous fruits. I assume such is generally true regardless of the ethnic origin of a missionary group, including the western entities. However, one thing I have noticed from the church growth movement in Korea is the sheer dedication of Koreans in general and Korean Christians in particular, and this is expressed not only in their actions but also in their prayer lives. In a way, Koreans are singly goal-oriented against a general cultural assumption that they are relation-oriented. In fact, they are both goal- and relationally oriented.

Cultural adaptation

As mentioned previously, those who grew up in a mono-cultural setting find it additionally challenging to adapt to another culture and cultural behavior. Thus, it not only takes more time, but also more effort to adjust to the host culture. At the same time, Korean missionaries, like those emerging from churches from the global South, have shared cultural traits that can be readily identified in the host cultures, unless they go to the West for their missionary vocation. This proximity is found also in their economic levels, so that the Korean missionaries find it easier to associate with nationals in their own homes and communities with much adjustment, even if there is considerable poverty. The Korean missionaries' experience during the economic difficulties can be another important source of identification with the nationals. They can easily sit with locals and enjoy unfamiliar food offered with less trouble and hesitation, use their primitive toilets, and sleep on the floors offered by local members. Considering the adjustments that Western missionaries have to make to establish a meaningful relationship through such participations, it is understandable to see how some Korean missionaries have been successful. The same is applied to most non-Western missionaries.

Also, an important resource is the divided state of the two Koreas and its continuing tensions. As many mission contexts include racial and religious conflicts, Koreans can empathise more realistically, with those

95

to whom they communicate God's message of reconciliation.

Spiritual life and prayer

As a Korean Christian, I am truly grateful for this
unique heritage. Korean Christians have learned that
prayer is the most powerful resource they have, when
they have no one to turn to in personal and national
crises. This applies to the harsh period of the Japanese
annexation of the country, the fierce Korean War when
Christians were a priority target along with public
servants, and the ensuing conflict across the border
between the two Koreas. This also applies to personal
and family settings during the struggling economic
hardships after the war and during the recovery from
the devastation. Hardships reinforced and strength-
ened Korean Christians' commitment to prayer life.
The presence of countless prayer mountains and
prayer houses throughout the country and among
immigrant Korean communities attests to this. It is
assumed that most missionaries continue this deep
spiritual tradition in their personal and church life.

Generosity

Korean churches are, by and large, giving churches.
Korean culture in general stresses hospitality and
generosity as an important virtue. Christian teaching
reinforces this cultural force and, as a result, Korean
Christians are known for their sacrificial giving
and hospitality. And this orientation has also been
characteristic of Korean mission. However, this also
requires cultural sensitivity and missionary implications. Dependency has been, from the very beginning

of the modern mission, the most pressing practical issue. There are many cases of impulsive giving among Korean Christians. For example, when they are impressed by the Holy Spirit or by the presentation of a need, their inner urge to give is so strong, they just give, only to occasionally regret it later. In spite of related problems, generosity, without a doubt, is an important gift of the Korean church. I firmly believe that God blesses generous hearts, and that is what Korean Christianity practices and experiences.

Missiological Implications

Several issues are raised in the form of questions to both the traditional and new missionary sending churches.

First, the very fundamental issue of definition still remains as the most important question in mission: What is mission? Without going into details, the Crusade model of mission seems to have remained consistent in mission forces, past and present. This model also assumes a definition that mission is "from the 'haves' to the 'have nots'." In a practical term, the object of the "haves" is far more than the Christian gospel: economy and civilization frequently precedes the gospel. That is, a missionary from a Christian-rich African nation working in Korea, for example, is not viewed as normal. This imperialistic model of mission is dangerously widespread among the people in the pew, and the new mission churches in the global South have unfortunately repeated this. There is no doubt that such a fundamental problem in turn affects almost every aspect of missionary activities including a hierarchical relationship between the missionary and national workers. The missionaries, partly because of their relatively rich resources and more importantly because of a wrong perception of mission itself, forget that they are to be guests to the host culture. If this is a critical issue, then what has motivated the sending bodies and individual missionaries to commit to mission?

Second, what is the level of cultural adaptation that is genuine and desirable for missionaries? Do they feel comfortable with the people and culture of the host country? When they use their hands to eat, do we also use our hands or look for a spoon? Do we always bring toilet paper or bottled water, when we visit mountain villages? And how does one feel about tricky cultural negotiations? More fundamentally, how do we practice incarnational lifestyle in bringing God's good news, knowing that the messenger is the most important part of his or her message?

Third, are you a good listener to the voice of God and that of newly adopted people? What is a right missionary attitude, one who is there to minister, or also ready to be ministered to? An effective missionary work requires a good two-way communication. A common tendency is to talk rather than to listen. In the same vein, the tendency is teach rather than to be taught. Do we impose our cultural practices and values? That is, does Korean missionary engagement smell of Kimchi? Do they approach the nationals with a big brother attitude? It is then critical to closely examine a 'partnership' between a missionary and nationals. Is it based on a mutual respect and appreciation of each other's gifts, resources and commitment, or a patronizing or even a hierarchical relationship? The latter two are not called 'partnership.'

Fourth, in a lived-out setting of our Christian and missionary conviction, what is the guiding principle? Ultimately what motivates missionaries to leave their familiar environment and move to an unknown place to live among people other than their own? With no hesitation, that is love. Let me read a South African Pioneer Missionary's Translation of 1 Corinthians 13.[16]

> If I have the language perfectly and speak like a native and have not his love, I am nothing.

> If I have diplomas and degrees and know all the up-to-date methods, and have not his touch of understanding love, I am nothing.

> If I am able to argue successfully against the religions of the people and make fools of them and have not his wooing of love, I am nothing.

> If I have all faiths and great ideals and magnificent plans and not his love that sweats and bleeds and weeps and prays and pleads, I am nothing.

> If I give my clothes and money to them and have not love for them, I am nothing.

> If I surrender all prospects, leave home and friends and make the sacrifices of a missionary career and then turn sour and selfish amid the daily annoyances and slights of the missionary life, then I am nothing.

---

16   Paul G. Hiebert, *Anthropological Insights for Missionaries*, Grand Rapids, MI: Baker Book House, p. 270.

If I can heal all manner of sickness and disease but wound hearts and hurt feelings for want of His love that is kind, I am nothing.

If I can write articles and publish books that win applause but fail to transcribe the word of the cross into the language of his love, I am nothing.

Fifth, what will then make it possible for missionaries from old and new mission churches (e.g., western and Asian churches) to work together? There are several areas of collaboration, and some of them are: 1) Being together for fellowship, networking and cooperation; 2) Sharing information and experiences, as the older partner comes with a rich deposit of experience, both positive and negative, while the new churches have new dynamics; 3) Bringing each other's needs, especially in mission operation, so that each other's gifts can complement each other, and ultimately the Kingdom's work; and 4) Creating spaces and occasions for both mission forces to come together for sharing with and learning from each other's experiences and traditions.

Conclusion

I have attempted to briefly present Korean mission with its strengths and weaknesses. However, because of its relatively short history, my observations and analysis are tentative. At the same time, the process of deep reflection is essential as the 'mid-course adjustment' should be done sooner rather than later. The list of strengths and weaknesses can continue further. Out of such an evaluative process, I have become deeply aware of God's 'risky' plan to use far-from-perfect people like Koreans and the Korean church. In humility, Korean mission communities, like many newer mission churches, have much to learn from the history of Western Christian missions. Even if Christianity, in general, and the missionary movement, in particular, has consistently decreased in the West, the Western church has much to offer in preparing the new churches for mission. If everyone is honest enough, the sharing of the West's missionary mistakes will be especially useful, so that the new mission churches will not have to repeat them. The emerging missionary churches can assist the weakening West by bringing their spiritual dynamics to its churches. To this end, the immigrant communities in the West have the potential to play a critical role in the re-shaping of global Christianity. With varying sets of gifts, both the West and the 'rest' are called to closely partner for God's mission. We are acutely reminded that mission is not ours but God's, and we are simply his partners.

Although there is a good place in Christian life and mission for military rhetoric, Jesus' incarnational mission is our ultimate model, not the infamous Crusade. Jesus 'won' the adversaries, not through his heavenly power, but through giving himself for others. His power was closely restricted to his love and humility. 'Mission in humility and hope' is a phrase used in a seminal document of Towards 2010 in the centenary celebration of the Edinburgh Missionary Conference.17 It is important to note that this is the reflective confession of a missionary leader of the Church of Scotland, which hosted the 1910 conference. If our mission is to conquer the land and bring a victory with our own strengths and strategies, I am afraid we may never stop the unfortunate historical cycle that will haunt the church with its self-crusading and self-glorifying goals.

May our Lord continue to use new missionary churches such as the Korean, as well as the old ones, for his kingdom. Yes, mission belongs neither to the new nor to the old church, neither to the West nor the 'rest'. It is God's. *Missio Dei.* .

Dr Julie Ma is a Research Tutor in Missiology with OCMS.

Looking Back to Move Forward

Some Lessons and Challenges from Mission History

Mark Laing

When my children attended primary school in India they dreaded the exam period—which seemed to recur rather frequently. They would have to endure a couple of weeks of written exams. For several nights before a particular test they would memorise, verbatim, the answers for particular questions in preparation for regurgitating this in the exam. One time my son came unstuck in a geography exam, his methodology failed him. After the exam he reported, "I knew all the answers, but I forgot which answer belonged to which question!"

When I taught missiology in India I sometimes encountered students who did not want to think about missiological questions, but, like school children, wanted set answers to standard questions. I kept saying to them: "there are no easy answers. In the particular situation you will find yourself in, you need to know: what are the key questions to ask?" Only when you know what are the right questions can you then develop appropriate answers. I say this by way of introduction—and perhaps excuse—because I come to you more with questions than with answers.

In this paper I want to consider some factors which affect the future of mission organisations and thus need to be considered for determining mission policy. For each factor I will do this by moving from historical examples to then examine what questions arise for us today. In turn, I would like to consider the role of finance in determining mission policy. I do that through the example of the correspondence between Lesslie Newbigin, as a newly arrived Church of Scotland missionary to India, and the General Secretary of the organisation, based in Edinburgh.

How does the big picture of socio-political events impact upon mission? I contrast the example of the growth of Christianity in Korea versus Japan, and then explore another Indian example. How did the changing political scene at the time of Indian Independence affect the "mass movements"?

For two hundred years Protestant missionary organisations operated with an assumed direction, from the West to the majority world. I ask whether the current organisations, bequeathed to us from this movement, can effectively serve as a conduit for mission in reverse.

We are on the eve of celebrating the centenary of the World Missionary Conference held in Edinburgh, in 1910. One of the consequences of that conference was the birth of the modern ecumenical movement.

In conclusion, I ask, what today does mission have to do with unity, or, more pointedly, disunity. To move forward, what are the lessons we need to learn from our recent ecumenical history?

The Role of Finance

Go ye into all the world and make disciples of all nations subject to budgetary requirements.

We are in the midst of the biggest financial crisis for at least a generation. Those of you who are involved in mission leadership will know better than I the impact the crisis is having on your organisation.[1] Does the financial crisis require that what we refer to as the great commission to be re-written? As Bishop Newbigin once quipped: "'Go ye into all the world and make disciples of all nations subject to budgetary requirements'. For our traditional mode of operation, a major evangelistic opening would be a major financial disaster".[2] Are we right to say, "more money, more ministry"[3] and consequently now—less money, less ministry?

I want to make a historical connection between our current financial woes and those of mission organisations during the late 1930s, when at that time they too faced severe financial constraints upon their

1   Gaines, S., "Fears over Credit Crunch Impact on Charity Donations.", http://www.guardian.co.uk/society/2008/jul/09/charities.creditcrunch?gusrc=rss&feed=society, 9 July, 2008, retrieved 1/6/2009.
2   Newbigin, J. E. L. "The Work of the Holy Spirit in the Life of the Asian Churches" in *A Decisive Hour for the Christian World Mission*. Norman Goodall and J. E. L. Newbigin, London: SCM Press, pp. 18-33.
3   Eskridge, L. and M. A. Noll (2000). *More Money, More Ministry: Money and Evangelicals in Recent North American History*, Grand Rapids: Eerdmans.

operations. For my PhD research I have been studying aspects of Lesslie Newbigin's life. As a young Church of Scotland missionary in rural Tamil Nadu there is a very interesting record of correspondence between Newbigin on the field and the secretary of the Church of Scotland Foreign Mission Committee (FMC), the Rev Dr Alexander Kydd based at 121 George Street.[4]

Kydd is the weary secretary who, year after year, presents his annual report to the General Assembly.[5] It is a tale of woe; the mission is in a dire financial situation, year on year the deficit is growing. In contrast the number of suitable candidates coming forward is dwindling. Kydd faces some very hard choices and the stress he is under takes a personal toll, forcing him to retire early due to ill health. The annual reports that Kydd presents to the General Assembly are not a pretty picture. From 1936 to 1945 there is retrenchment, reduced numbers of missionaries, problems in recruiting missionaries and accumulative financial deficits, which, because of their persistent nature, cause the FMC to even consider the total abandonment of one of its fields, or else across the board reduction to their work. Does this sound similar to today's scenario!? Kydd's reports continue to harken back to the more abundant years of the early 1930s trying to awaken a declining home church to the growth of the "younger churches", and the FMC's resultant responsibility.

4   Most of this correspondence is in Accession 7548, Box 130, of the Foreign Mission Records of the Church of Scotland, at the National Library of Scotland, George IV Bridge, Edinburgh, EH1 1EW, UK.
5   For Kydd's annual report see the respective: "Report of the Foreign Mission Committee." In *Reports to the General Assembly with the Legislative Acts*. The General Assembly of the Church of Scotland. Edinburgh: W. Blackwood, 1936- 1946.

More importantly however, these reports provide an insight into the mission policy of the FMC (particularly that expressed by the general secretary) and the adaptation of that policy to a changing context at home and abroad. As you know the world was changing very rapidly during this time with the growth of nationalism and rapid de-colonisation. Kydd's response throughout this time is to plead for more money to the assembly. If we only had more money then we could continue to do what we had successfully done in the past—run our vast array of mission institutions.

Repeatedly the FMC appeals to the Scottish churches to preserve its financial well-being, the assumption being that if the FMC can attain sound financial footing, and recruit adequate personnel, it therefore has the warrant to continue its existing mission policies regardless of the changing context on the "field". For Kydd finances rather than events on the field dictated the future direction of the FMC. If finances could be procured to avert the current crisis then the status quo of current mission policy could be maintained. The FMC's missionary endeavour remains locked into maintaining their institutional heritage, any departure from such "sound methods" being deemed "disastrous". The current role and practice of the FMC is essential to the field, and despite financial constraints should be perpetuated.

Repeated failure on both fronts eventually prepares the FMC for a more fundamental reassessment of its relationship to the "younger church". These factors, combined with a rapidly changing context during the war years, the rise of nationalism, and the growing voice of the "younger church", force the FMC to reassess its role, the rationale being that these circumstances, rather than being understood as adverse, should be perceived as being providential to guide the FMC in the evolution of its relationship with the "younger churches". This marked a fundamental change of focus for the FMC, from the past to the future, from the mission to the indigenous church.

Newbigin, the young, enthusiastic missionary in rural India saw things quite differently.[6] In his letters home and to Kydd, rather than the financial woes of the mission, Newbigin's attention is grabbed by the profound growth of the indigenous church, and what he described as the "spontaneous expansion of the church".[7] In contrast to prevalent missionary attitudes which saw the urban institutional work of the mission as being central, Newbigin recognises that what was considered peripheral—the village work—should be given central priority to facilitate "building up the church in the only place where it is growing".[8] Newbigin's basic orientation was to the "only" place of church growth—the village. At the start of his tenure as a district missionary he intimated a fundamental shift away from maintaining the mission institutions,

6 After language study Newbigin was district missionary in Kanchipuram, Tamil Nadu, from 1936-1946.

7 Newbigin, J. E. L., *A South India Diary (Revised Edition)*. London: SCM Press, 1960.

8 Letter, Newbigin to Kydd 27/12/1939, Acc7548/ B130.

to serving and equipping the local church, in this instance through lay leadership training and developing the role of women.

Newbigin saw the financial crisis as an opportunity to realign the mission to the village church and, in so doing, jettison some institutional obligations, Kydd sees the future much more bleakly, the future of the mission being intimately bound with the future of "the country and Empire".[9]

Kydd and the FMC did not read the situation well. Their response on how they should relate to the indigenous church which they had birthed came only when their hands were forced by financial constraints. It is easy for us to recognise the mistakes of our predecessors. To look back and say, it was obvious, they should have made those changes. The questions we face are not that same 70 years on but are we doing any better today? How are we responding to the financial crisis? What role does declining finance and recruitment have in changing our mission policy? Do we see the financial downturn not as a threat to mission operations but as an opportunity for change? And, if so, a change in what direction?

A related issue is the necessity of educating supporters during these days of change. Why do people support missions? How do we maintain the loyalty of our supporters when faced with the need to make changes? Or does the need to maintain supporters also mean that we keep doing what is expected of us?

9   Letter, Kydd to Newbigin 3/2/1940, Acc7548/A23.

Another important issue which arises from this historical case is the relationship between "young Turk" missionary and senior missionary statesman. How are decision made? Hudson Taylor, with the CIM, was the first to devolve decision-making to the field, away from the UK home base. For a mission organisation to make a major change in direction are the structures there for the mission to adequately discern the voice of God? In decision making which voices have most weight?

The Big Picture: "You in your small corner and I in mine" [10]

Planning mission policy and strategizing is often done with the focus primarily on the mission agency. When this is done two important aspects are often neglected, the larger socio-political climate, and the role and place of the recipients of the gospel. The reception of Christianity is related to how it is perceived by those assessing it. Who is bearing the message, and what is their relationship to the dominant political power? What is their place in society? Concerning the big picture I want to give two examples of how context can directly impact the outcome of mission. The first example contrasts the response to the gospel in Japan with Korea; the second example is from India.

Korea and Japan

The percentage of Christians in South Korea is about 32% of the total population whereas in Japan it stands at just over 1%.[11] Why such a difference given

10   From hymn, "Jesus Bids Us Shine" by Susan Bogert Warner.
11   "South Korea" and "Japan", http://www.operationworld.org, accessed 1/6/2008.

the sincere and industrious efforts of missionaries in both countries? In comparing Korea and Japan the pre-World War II role played by America is critical. Korea was faced with the threat of Japanese colonialism. In these circumstances many Koreans discovered that Christianity "provided an 'oppositional ideology' for resisting the Japanese government", with many Christians being involved in nationalist movements; in spite of the fact that the gospel presented by missionaries in Korea was "apolitical" and stressed "personal salvation and piety".[12]

> [C]ircumstances beyond the control of any mission strategist led to the positive linkage between Christianity and Korean cultural identity and provided the basis for the remarkable post-war growth of Christianity in Korea. This transformation of "perception" did not occur in Japan, because the source of Christianity was also the source of Japan's greatest enemy".[13]

Christianity came as a friend to Korea's liberation (from Japan), but as a foe to Japan. We can assume that the missionaries to Japan were just as spiritual, just as zealous and committed as those to Korea. But today there is a stark difference between almost a third of the population being Christian versus just over 1%. We can see with hindsight that significant to the reception of the gospel was the way America was perceived. Where we are working we need to understand the big picture today.

12 Mullins, M. R., "Christianity Transplanted" in M. R. Mullins and R. F. Young, *Perspectives on Christianity in Korea and Japan: The Gospel and Culture in East Asia.* Lampeter, Edwin Mellen Press, 1995, p. 73.
13 ibid.

Predating the above example is the case of the reception of Christianity by dalits in India and by the various tribes in the north east. Christians account for about 3% of the total population but, like butter on toast, they are not evenly spread across the nation. In parts of the north east, such as Nagaland, nearly 90% of the population would claim to be Christian, and about 20% in South India, but in what is known as the Hindu heartland the percentage of Christians can be less than 0.1%. Why these disparities? Most Christian communities are descended from what are referred to as mass movements. Dalits and tribal people, oppressed by Bhramminical Hinduism, sought liberation and aligned themselves to the foreign occupying power and their faith, the British and Christianity. Those with most to gain embraced Christianity whilst those with most to lose, the caste Hindus, largely resisted Christianity. Christianity was—and to some extent still is—regarded as a foreign faith and the Indian Christian community were viewed as an appendage of the missionaries.[14] During the struggle for Indian Independence Ghandi interpreted mass conversion to Christianity by the dalits as a political act and he indicated that he would use political means to block it.[15]

> "The price of gaining political freedom from the British Raj would be that religious minorities had to conform to the Hindu majority, and therefore conversion would be severely constrained". (Kim 2003:34-5).

14   Kim, S. C. H. *In Search of Identity: Debates on Religious Conversion in India.* New Delhi, New York: Oxford University Press, 2003, p. 34.
15   ibid., pp. 34-35.

From Independence on various laws were passed to limit or halt the mass movements.

Hindu objections to conversion have been concretized in three main ways: by the introduction of Hindu 'personal laws', which were disadvantageous for caste Hindus who converted to another religion (1955–6); by the limitation of social benefits for converts from Scheduled Caste backgrounds (1950s); and by the passing of the 'freedom of religion acts' in various states (1960s and 70s).[16]

These laws worked, effectively blocking mass conversion and halting these movements to Christianity. What happened in the socio-political sphere, piloted by Ghandi, is particularly important because during that time a young American missionary, Donald McGavran, was trying to initiate a mass movement amongst the Satnami caste in Madhya Pradesh. McGavran wrote:

> [F]or the next eighteen years I devoted myself to the evangelization of one caste, the Satnamis. I wish that I could record that I was hugely successful but this is not the case. Perhaps 1000 individuals were won to Christian faith but no castewide movement to Christ resulted. By 1950 accessions [conversions] from that caste had almost ceased. True, there were fifteen new small village churches but the movement had stopped.[17]

McGavran writes that out of this the basic theory and theology of the Church Growth Movement (CGM) emerged, being "hammered out on the anvil of

16   Kim, S. C. H. and K. Kim, *Christianity as a World Religion*, London and New York: Continuum, 2008, p. 195.
17   McGavran, D. A., *Church Growth and Group Conversion*, Pasadena: William Carey Library, 1973, p. 56.

experience".[18] He claimed that "The principles underlying the Indian case histories presented are timeless and apply to many lands....Group conversion from within a people applies all round the world".[19] McGavran and the CGM persisted in arguing pragmatically that, if certain principles for creating people movements were observed, great church growth would ensue. McGavran developed his theories on the back of JW Pickett's study.[20] But he failed to understand the big picture. Conversion had become politicized; Ghandi had shifted the goal posts to effectively halt these movements.[21]

Again, with the benefit of hindsight it is easy for us to be critical of McGavran, in failing to see the bigger political picture. For us today, beyond our mission policies, what aspects of the socio-political context help or hinder people from coming to Christ? How do we develop the eyes to interpret these factors? Should mission policy be adapted in light of the socio-political context?

18   McGavran cited by Pinola, S., *Church Growth: Principles and Praxis of Donald A. McGavran's Missiology*. Åbo: Åbo Akademi University Press, 1995, p. 75.

19   McGavran, D. A., *Church Growth and Group Conversion*, Pasadena: William Carey Library, 1973, pp. x-xi.

20   Pickett, J. W., Christian Mass Movements in India: A Study with Recommendations. New York: Abingdon Press, 1933, and Pickett, J. W., *Mass Movement Survey Report for Mid-India*, Mission Press, 1936.

21   See Laing, M. T. B., "The Consequences of the 'Mass Movements'." *Indian Church History Review* 35(2), pp. 91-104 and Laing, M. T. B., "Donald McGavran's Missiology: An Examination of the Origins and Validity of Key Aspects of the Church Growth Movement." *Indian Church History Review* 36(1), pp. 30-52.

For nearly forty years Newbigin worked as a missionary in South India. When he "retired" to Britain Newbigin was often been asked: "What is the greatest difficulty you face in moving from India to England?" Newbigin's answer was always the same, "The disappearance of hope [from western society]."[22]

After nearly 40 years of missionary experience in India Newbigin could say of the West, "Here, without possibility of question, is the most challenging missionary frontier of our time".[23] Hope has disappeared and the West has rejected Christianity and turned to a form of paganism which actively resists the gospel. In the West Newbigin found "a paganism born out of the rejection of Christianity [which] is far tougher and more resistant to the Gospel than the pre-Christian paganisms with which foreign missionaries have been in contact during the past 200 years". [24]

With over 200 years of experience in training and equipping people to take the gospel cross-culturally to others what is the role of mission societies today in reaching the post-modern, post-Christian West? Western mission societies are uniquely placed to equip the Western church which has largely failed to be missionary, but has thought of mission in terms of foreign mission. That is not a new question.

22   Newbigin, J. E. L., *The Other Side of 1984: Questions for the Churches*, Geneva: WCC Publications, 1983, p. 1.
23   Newbigin, J. E. L., "Can the West Be Converted?" *Princeton Seminary Bulletin*, 6(1), pp. 25-37.
24   ibid., p. 36.

In the 1980s Professor Wilbert Shenk interviewed all the major mission agencies in Europe (including UK). He wanted to find out if the lessons learned from those 200 years of missions could be utilised for mission to the West. Shenk travelled Europe asking two questions: What was attitude of old established mission agencies with regard to mission to the West? Most had a charter for foreign mission. Did the mission agency have any training programmes in the West dedicated to training missionaries to approach modern western culture and work in their own country? All the mission agencies gave that same answer—no, we don't do anything regarding mission to the West. Shenk's second question was simple: Ought there to be? All said yes there should be. Shenk realized that it was a time of inertia, churches were in decline, but unsure of what ought to be done. Churches were totally unprepared. Denominations admitted they were in trouble, but had no imagination, no will to try something new. Shenk recognised the need for new missiological foundations rather than repeat the mistakes of past missionary training, which was "by the seat of your pants" (or trousers, depending on what side of the Atlantic you are on!).[25]

I know this is not main concern for this conference but I want to ask you the question that Shenk asked over twenty years ago—what are you doing to equip the western church to engage missiologically with western society? How are mission agencies today facilitating what missionaries referred to as the "blessed reflex"?—allowing the growth and the vitality of the church in the majority to revive the flagging

25   Shenk, W., interview with Mark Laing, 1/11/06, Pune.

Christianity of the West. As General Simatoupong of Indonesia asked, "Of course, the Number One question is, Can the West be converted?"[26]

In 1988, the Lausanne (LCWE European) Committee met for a conference in Stuttgart, where "All agreed that the spiritual paralysis within the churches is the greatest obstacle to the evangelization of Europe's spiritually hungry millions". In order to rectify this situation they gave a call, reminiscent of the Macedonian Call:

> Come over and help us! We Christians in Europe confess that we need to learn from the churches in Africa, Asia, and the Americas in their unself-conscious, winsome ways of sharing the abundant life of Christ. So we invite the church worldwide to work with us in partnership for the re- evangelization of our continent and the still unreached.[27]

We know that many missionaries have come (and are coming) to the West. But are mission agencies ready for mission in reverse; to be a conduit for mission from the majority world to the West, a complete reversal of the historical direction of Protestant mission. This is important for missionaries and for missionary training.

Training for Mission: the Unnamed
from Cyprus and Cyrene

"Christianity is spread primarily by local believers and developed by them in local ways. Attention to the

26   Newbigin, J. E. L., *The Gospel and Our Culture*, London: Catholic Missionary Education Centre, 1990, p. 13.
27   Cited in Glasser, A. F., "Mission in the 1990s: Two Views." *International Bulletin of Missionary Research* 13(1), 1989, pp. 2-10.

activities of foreign missionaries has tended to obscure this fact...", that Christianity primarily spreads "from below."[28] The biographies of missionaries and the histories of mission societies give us a biased account of the spread of Christianity, hogging the limelight. But it has been repeatedly attested that those most effective at propagating the faith are local believers, who are often unseen, untrained and unnamed.

Paul gets the limelight in the Book of Acts. But the very significant work of crossing the huge cultural barrier, breaking out of Judaism to preach to Gentiles was by unnamed men from Cyprus and Cyrene (Acts 11:19-21). And within a few chapters in the book of Acts the centre for Christianity moves from Jerusalem to Antioch.[29]

> "Christians today move around the world as the first Christians moved around the Roman Empire— for employment, as slaves, as domestic servants and due to persecution. As they do they spread their faith. One of the unforeseen consequences of contemporary globalization may be the further spread of Christianity from below."[30]

What is our response to this diaspora of Christians scattered around the world, with some Christians placed in very strategic places such as in gulf countries?

28   Kim, S. C. H. and K. Kim, *Christianity as a World Religion*. London/New York: Continuum, 2008, pp. 211-212.

29   Laing, M. T. B., "The Changing Face of Mission: Implications for the Southern Shift in Christianity." *Missiology* 34(2), 2006, pp. 165-177.

30   Kim, S. C. H. and K. Kim, *Christianity as a World Religion*. London/New York: Continuum, 2008, p. 212.

Dr Walter Hollenweger was professor of mission at the University of Birmingham in Britain (1971-89), and simultaneously taught at the Selly Oak Colleges. In a personal reflection on his career Hollenweger recalled, and contrasted, his experience of training future missionaries, with that of teaching majority world students. Of the missionary candidates he wrote:

> Most of them were well-meaning young people with rather weak educational backgrounds, especially regarding their language capacities, but with strong convictions about being 'called' to missionary work.... They believed with all their hearts that their conversion experience and their British understanding of the New Testament were sufficient preparation for missionary work — a catastrophic misunderstanding when confronted with the situation overseas. [31]

Regarding majority world students he recalled that "typically were better educated than the missionary candidates".[32] Through these and other experiences he came to the following conclusion about missionary training:

> because mission is about church growth, we must invest our resources in indigenous evangelists, pastors, and theologians, who can do the job better and cheaper than Westerners. This fact is slowly but surely dawning on some mission societies. Moreover, in many places of the world the departure of missionaries has given the indigenous churches an important evangelistic impetus.[33]

31   Hollenweger, W. J., "My Pilgrimage in Mission," *International Bulletin of Missionary Research*, 29(2), 2005, p.87.
32   ibid.
33   ibid.

Another conclusion he arrived at was that now the West was receiving this "blessed reflex" as a consequence of the global spread of majority world Christians:

> because mission has to do with our ecumenical calling, we ought to begin now at our doorsteps. The Lord has sent us hundreds of missionaries from the Third World. They are the direct or indirect product of our mission efforts. Now they come back to us in the form of immigrants, refugees, and foreign students.... They help us in understanding our ecumenical calling. They might also vitalize our worn-out Christianity.[34]

There is opportunity and responsibility to give and receive. The western church needs humility to learn of the profound syncretism of western culture with the gospel. The combination of enlightenment ideals with Christianity has produced a church timid in its witness, relegated and privatized by society, complacent about it fragmentation into many divisions, and without the will or knowledge of how to change, how to be missionary in western society. In the West we need to relearn our ecclesiology, how the church embodies God's mission to the world. And we can do that, not be looking back to the glory days of past Christendom, but by learning from those who come to the West from vibrant dynamic churches.

The migration of majority world Christians to the West for a variety of reasons presents us with challenges and opportunities.[35] Opportunities which

34   ibid, p. 88.
35   Hanciles, J. (2003). "Migration and Mission: Some Implications for the Twenty-First-Century Church," *International Bulletin of Mission-*

mission agencies are more strategically placed to respond to and serve as a channel for the blessing of the churches.

First, how do we provide training for the vibrant Christians who come with a very wide range of needs and abilities? The West, with its heritage of theological education and vast resources has responsibility to provide ongoing training to the most able in the majority world. Of course there is always the danger that many trained in the West will not return to the majority world to develop theological education there. And there is also the danger notably of American colleges cherry-picking the best from the majority world to serve on their teaching faculty. The second issue concerns those from the majority world who stay on in the West. How can the Western church be renewed through them? It seems that the "mainline" churches and, for example, the African Diaspora are passing each other by, like ships in the night.

Mission and (Dis)Unity

"The ecumenical movement was in large part the outgrowth of the missionary movement."[36]

"Comity, conference, and co-operation became common practice on the mission fields. And in due course this had its effect upon the sending churches."[37]

ary Research, 27(4), 2003. pp. 146-150, 152-153.

36 Latourette, K. S., "Ecumenical Bearings of the Missionary Movement and the International Missionary Council," in R. Rouse and S. Neill, *A History of the Ecumenical Movement, 1517-1948*, London: Ecumenical Institute/SPCK, 1954, p. 353

37 Newbigin, J. E. L., "Unity and Mission." *Covenant Quarterly* 19, 1961, pp. 3-6.

We are on the eve of celebrating Edinburgh 2010. In doing so we look back at the missionary conference held in Edinburgh in 1910. The very pragmatic Edinburgh conference explored avenues for better cooperation in mission. This was not from any theological impetus towards unity but from the compelling motive of evangelism, the conference delegates, under the influence of the chairman, John R Mott, adopting the Student Volunteer Movement for Foreign Missions slogan, "the evangelization of the world in this generation," as their own watchword. The main contribution of Edinburgh towards the relationship between mission and unity came from what Edinburgh constituted rather that from what actually took place at the conference. In constituting a continuation committee Edinburgh "ensured that international and inter-denominational missionary cooperation should move from the stage of occasional conferences to that of continuous and effective consultation."[38]

As a result of the ecumenical movement in the twentieth century the church underwent a major revision of its ecclesiology challenging the assumptions inherited from a defective and now redundant Christendom ecclesiology. This combined with two other factors, the demise of Christendom, and the missionary encounters of western Christianity with the non-western world,[39] brought us to what was referred to as a recovery of ecclesiology. We recovered an understanding that the church has a dual calling

38   Newbigin, J. E. L., "Co-Operation and Unity." *International Review of Mission* 59(233), pp. 67-74.
39   Newbigin, J. E. L., *The Household of God: Lectures on the Nature of the Church*, London: SCM Press, 1953, pp. 1-25.

to mission and to unity and that these aspects are inextricably bound together.

One of our biggest problems in the history of Protestant missions has been the separation of mission from the church. The church is understood as a community called out of the world to worship God and nurture believers. Mission is delegated to specialist organisations which take the gospel to the ends of the earth, and plant churches. Ralph Winter made the claim that one of the biggest failings of missions has been not to take that extra step beyond planting the church, to establish mission organisations.[40] I think Winter is wrong in advocating that we perpetuate this dichotomy between mission and the church. The Protestant missionary movement, with the advent of mission societies is a historical peculiarity, which emerged because of the failure of the western church. Our biggest failing has been our failure to grasp that the church is God's mission to the world. We hold onto outdated, irrelevant models of the church rather than seek to embody the missionary nature of the church. And this separation between mission organisations and churches continues to be detrimental to both.

Bishop Newbigin, with many others, argued that church unity which was tangible and locally visible, belonged to the true nature of the church and the demonstration of this unity was essential for the effective witness of the church. He understood the two as emanating from the heart of the Gospel and as therefore essential to the dual calling of the church:

40   Winter, R. D., "Ghana: Preparation for Marriage." International Review of Mission, 67(267), 1978, pp. 339-340; c.f. ch. 1, p. 24 of this book.

>"The connection between the movement for Christian reunion and the movement for world evangelization is of the deepest possible character. The two things are the two outward signs of a return to the heart of the Gospel itself."[41]

It is not possible to account for the contentment with the divisions of the Church except upon the basis of a loss of the conviction that the Church exists to bring all men to Christ. There is the closest possible connection between the acceptance of the missionary obligation and the acceptance of the obligation of unity. That which makes the Church one is what makes it a mission to the world.[42]

That which God has joined together, let no-one separate. The whole ecumenical movement, the quest to recover the unity of the church, is a product of the missionary movement. But, as evangelicals, we have a terrible track record of holding together what God has joined together. Take for instance the mission theology of the Lausanne movement versus Geneva (the CWME), which for decades polarized thinking into either camp, one which understand proclamation as primary, the other which held to humanization. If mission and unity belong to the heart of the gospel then our effectiveness in mission is profoundly undermined by our divisions and fragmentation. Jesus, in his high priestly prayer, prayed that we might be one so that the world might believe that Christ has been sent by his Father (John 17:20-3). Near the end of his life Newbigin wrote that "nothing can remove from the Gospel the absolute imperative of unity. I am sure that, for so

41 Newbigin, J. E. L., *The Reunion of the Church: A Defence of the South India Scheme*, London: SCM Press, 1960, p. 19.
42 ibid, p. 11.

long as I have breath, I must continue to confess my belief that God intends his Church to be ... 'an outward, visible and united society'."[43]

What are the practical implications of this in our work for world mission today? Can we continue as evangelicals with our two mandate approach? We, as evangelicals, have a mandate for world mission, and ecumenicals can get on with their discussions on church unity—and neither the two shall meet. This denies our recent history, that ecumenism arose out of the missionary movement and must continue to inform it.

Conclusion

I have looked at various historical examples with the hope that rather than repeat the mistakes of history, we will learn from them. For the Church of Scotland in the late 1930s the signs of a deteriorating home church were manifest in declining interest in mission expressed by reduced giving and missionary numbers. In contrast, on the field in South India, there was tremendous growth in the village churches. But this was largely independent of a mission shackled to its institutions. The historical inertia of the Church of Scotland made it difficult to turn the juggernaut to change direction. At that time, whilst Kydd looked backwards, others, with more prescience looked forward. In preparation for the Tambaram Conference (1938) Hendrick Kraemer stated that "the Church is always in a state of crisis and that its greatest shortcoming is that it is only occasionally aware of it. The

43   Newbigin, J. E. L., *Unfinished Agenda: An Updated Autobiography*, Geneva: WCC Publications, 1993, p. 253.

Church ought always to be aware of its condition of crisis on account of the abiding tension between its essential nature and its empirical condition."[44] Kydd wanted to maintain his course, the status quo, by fine tuning the sails. But what was needed was a completely different change in tack, a fundamental change in direction.

Further north, in the state of Madhya Pradesh McGavran was focused on starting a mass movement amongst the Satnami caste. He did not recognise the clouds gathering on the horizon which would halt the whole progress of mass conversions across India. More recently Shenk and Hollenweger highlighted that, although mission organisations recognised a crucial opportunity, they failed to capitalise on it.

For us today are we too focused on the immediate crises and demands, on our own responsibilities? Can we also see the horizon, read the signs of the times and respond appropriately (Matt. 16:2-3)? Are we seeking to hold the same course despite the weather, or is it time to change tack? Are we aware that the church "is always in a state of crisis"?

Our traditional focus on mission organisations and missionaries has obscured the fact that "Christianity is spread primarily by local believers."[45] The church is the mission; the church is God's mission to the world. How then can we heal the rift that has developed

44   Kraemer, H., *The Christian Message in a Non-Christian World*, London: Edinburgh House, 1938, pp.24-25.

Press.
45   Kim, S. C. H. and K. Kim, *Christianity as a World Religion*. London/New York: Continuum, 2008, p. 211.

between mission and church? There is always a time-lag between our theology and the embodiment of that theology. Historically Protestant mission had a poorly developed ecclesiology. We galloped ahead of the church eager to do mission, without the appropriate ability to think missiologically.

During the twentieth century we gradually recovered the relationship between our thinking and praxis. But now we have the opposite problem. We are not galloping ahead of our missiological thinking but lagging behind it. Our structures and institutions are too static, hindering the proper embodiment of our theological formulations.[46] We are locked into particular patterns of doing mission and being church because of our historical legacy. We now have an adequate theology of missionary ecclesiology, what is required is its proper embodiment.[47] In this the role of mission organisations is critical, as bearers of the missionary impulse, to re-educate the churches and overcome this ongoing dichotomy between mission and church. Could 2010 be the opportunity for the creative advance that Edinburgh 1910 was?

Mark Laing taught missiology at Union Biblical Seminary, Pune, India for several years, where his also directed the Centre for Mission Studies. He has recently completed doctoral studies at the University of Edinburgh.

46   c.f. Newbigin, J. E. L., "Anglicans, Methodists and Intercommunion: A Moment for Decision." *Churchman* 82(4), 1968, p. 282.
47   Laing, M. T. B., "Missio Dei: Some Implications for the Church." *Missiology* 37(1), 2009, pp. 89-99.

Equipping and Resourcing of Asian Mission Movements

Jacob Thomas

> From long and painful experience the Church in Asia-Pacific has learned one thing: mission is not political, economic, and least of all ecclesiastical colonialism which is brought from outside into "mission areas"; be it from the West or be it now from the North.[1]

May I invite you to New Delhi, November (5-8) 1999 when Pope Johannes Paulus II, on his second visit to India, made the following remarks: "The peoples of Asia need Jesus Christ and his Gospel. Asia is thirsting for the Living Water that Jesus alone can give." Such bold assertions, as critics described them, understandably raised quite a stir in India. On the 7th of November, after offering floral tributes at the Samadhi (final resting place) of Mahatma Gandhi, he wrote in the guest book of the memorial that "A culture cannot survive if it attempts to be exclusive." This quote borrowed from Gandhi, was personally signed as Johannes Paulus II. The next day, November 8, during the Papal High Mass he stated, "The First millennium saw the Cross planted in the soil of Europe and the Second in America and Africa. May the Third Christian Millennium witness a great harvest of faith on this vast and vital continent."

1   Michael T. Siegel and Leonardo N. Mercado, "The Status of Mission in the Asia- Pacific Region in *Towards An Asian Theology of Mission*, (eds. Seigel and Mercado) Manila: Divine Word Publications, 1995, p. 16.

Some in India insisted that this was part of the 'secret agenda' of aggressive Christian imperialism towards evangelisation and conversion of the peoples of Asia.[2]

Such reactions and responses, rather typical within Asia, help us identify the ongoing 'love-hate' relationship of Gospel and Culture in different parts of Asia. The proactive 'love relationship' unravels an outstanding history of transforming mission while the growing opposition unleashes violence even in a secular [equal rights to every religion] democratic country like India. Links with a 'Christian' colonial past reinforces the hostility towards Christianity which is viewed as an alien corrupting influence that exploited several Asian cultures and societies.

As these two streams—openness to the Gospel and forces of resistance—flow through Asian societies, the creative dynamic of the Gospel can emerge as a positive influence. Such a positive influence, I believe, is what enables the community of faith to remain strong 'even when the way goes through Death Valley,' (Ps.23, The Message). Persecution against faith communities, history teaches us, has also the potential of transforming communities into 'creational microcosms': "a resistance movement against prevailing patterns of idolatry and the corruption of personhood and community that stems from it."[3] While some of these issues might be equally relevant in Africa and Latin America, undoubtedly, the Asian context poses unique contextual challenges and issues. These criti-

2   http://www.southasiaanalysis.org/%5cpapers%5cpaper91. html accessed on 15 May 2010.

3   Andrew Perriman, Re:Mission : Biblical mission for a post-biblical church Paternoster, 2007, p.152.

cal challenges must inform/influence Asian Mission movements as they commit in partnership with the Spirit to let God's transforming word become truly incarnate in contemporary Asia.

For purposes of this paper I follow the definitional framework suggested by Kang San Tan. What is being attempted here is only a general overview related to Asia. There is a limitation that the discussion does not dig deeper into the specifics of the challenges that different national missionary movements within Asia encounter. This paper is also not able to give due attention to what creative expressions such as Faith to Faith, South Asia Concern, along with several other mission groups, are attempting to do in relating the Gospel to the multi-faith context of Britain, particularly to British Asians.

Asian Mission Movements

The term Asian Mission Movements (AMMs) refers to various Asian churches, mission structures, indigenous mission organizations, and alliances that seek to spread the gospel cross culturally, both within and beyond national boundaries. AMMs do not necessarily comprise a centralised or organised network but consist of many local communities—churches and indigenous groups engaged in cross cultural witness. In reflecting on the AMMs, there are at least two caveats.

First, the danger of Asian ethnocentrism, which claims that this is the Asia Pacific's Century, and that leadership in mission belongs to the Asian church. The reality is that Christ's mission is the concern of the whole church from all six continents. The AMMs need the contribution from a broader, international, and missiological community, recognising that there is much that newer missions can learn from "Older Sending Nations".

Second, one needs to be careful of the tendency to generalise Asian missionary movements as a single stream, thus overlooking the unique stages and distinct characteristics of each national missionary movement.[4]

An overview of the context of Asia

Asia is the world's largest and most populous continent with approximately 4 billion people constituting 60% of the world's current population. From the standpoint of mission it is important to highlight that the continent is set in the context of the major living religions of the world with the numerical paucity of Christians, truly a little flock making up barely three percent of the population. The linguistic, cultural, ethnic and religious diversity of the region, perhaps the highest concentration in the world—and the juxtaposition of highly developed and wealthy economies and mass poverty make it truly complex. The diversity is characteristic of almost each of the countries in the region.

4   Kang San Tan, "Who is in the Driver's Seat? A critique of mission partnership models between Western missions and East Asian mission movements". (See chapter 3.)

As Asia comes under the ever advancing globalising trends, rapid urbanisation is triggering the migration trends from rural areas to giant cities—by 2025 it is estimated that eighty percent of the world's population will be living in megapolises—"...tomorrow's flash points, the upheavals of the world will happen in the cities."[5]

In addition, poverty, deprivation and oppression are the common lot of the masses; structural evil with rampant corruption and natural disasters like typhoons, earthquakes, cyclones and tsunamis routinely cause devastation. The Church in Asia is fundamentally called to bring good news to the poor. Against such a bleak backdrop, AMMs have a distinct role to let the light of Jesus Christ's Gospel shine upon the dark clouds; the more we immerse ourselves into the context of Asia the better is our perception of the hopes and aspirations of this continent.

Having described the context in broad strokes, this paper identifies three specific aspects of the complex landscape within which AMMS are placed: 1. Cultural and Religious milieu, 2. Cultural Transition and the struggle for Cultural identity, 3. The Marginalised Poor.

From the point of view of the poor, some will insist that cultural and religious pluralism is not a major issue. Pluralism and religious dialogue is apparently a middle class agenda. The poor in their struggle for liberation engage in common praxis, overcoming the

5   Benigno P. Beltran, *Towards An Asian Theology of Mission*, Manila: Divine Word Publications, 1995, p. viii. For a fuller discussion see his article, "Proclaiming the Good News to the City", 87-93.

semantics that bother the rich, educated and the middle class. The pertinent challenge for mission is to talk about God by overcoming the limitation of the human structures of language.[6]

In highlighting the importance of these three aspects for missions in Asia, The Federation of Asian (Catholic) Bishops Conference insisted on a Dialogue of Life: dialogue with religions, dialogue with culture and dialogue with the poor.[7]

Cultural and Religious Milieu

A question that is often asked is whether there is a common defining element for Asia. The Asian milieu is more of a conglomeration of cultures and subcultures. Scholars will want to insist that there is no uniform reality of Asia—Asia does not have a single culture. Cultural, linguistic and religious diversity with each of the countries within the region is a characteristic that highlights the deep rooted cultural and religious pluralism of Asia. Asia is diversified into at least seven linguistic zones, the highest that any continent can boast.[8]

To cite just one example, Indonesia with over 13,000 islands has around 400 languages. Its vast

6   M.P.Joseph who teaches Social Ethics and Philosophy at one of the largest universities in Taiwan, Chang Jung Christian University, in a personal email to me insisted on this view point.

7   Rosales and Arévalo, (eds.) *For All the Peoples of Asia; Federation of Asian Bishops' Conference Documents from 1970-1991*, Quezon City: Claretian Publications, 1992.

8   Aloysius Pieris, "Towards an Asian Theology of Liberation. Some Religio-cultural Guidelines", p. 235-253, see section "Linguistic Heterogeneity", p 240ff in Douglas Elwood, (ed.) *Asian Christian Theology* Maryknoll: Orbis Books, 1980.

ethnic, cultural and religious diversity includes Islam as the majority religion, Hinduism of Bali, Kebatinan (essentially part of Javanese culture spread widely throughout Indonesia) part of Protestants, Catholics and Buddhists. Within the cultural and religious pluralism of Asia, there is bound to be an 'interactive pluralism'—Christians intermingle with 'neighbours' of other faiths. It is virtually impossible for mission movements in Asia to be isolated or insulated from the cultural, religious milieu.

Today Asian religions are vibrant, they go through a process of revival and reform often accompanied by fundamentalism and communalism. "The great Asian religions have elaborate philosophical, theological, liturgical, catechetical and ethical systems that answer to basic religious questions and satisfy the spiritual needs of their followers. They have a self-sufficient soteriological character...."[9] Karotemprel, professor at the Universita Urbaniana, Rome, continues to argue that Hinduism and Buddhism, often mistakenly perceived to be confined to particular geographical areas, are now universal religions. Along with their claims of having unique explanations and answers to the human predicament, they are making serious inroads in the West effectively reaching out to those that are drawn to Asian spirituality and cultures. Islam too is aggressively surging forward with its own vision of a pan-Islamic international order.[10]

Christian Mission of the future will have to take seriously such evaluations of the socio-religious phe-

9 Sebastian Karotemprel, "The Shape of Christian Mission in the Third Millennium" *Dharma Deepika*, January 2000, p. 53.

10 ibid, p. 52.

nomena pertaining to the context of Asia. Here is a specific challenge in our commitment to equip and resource the indigenous churches of Asia:

> Post-independent resurgence of national cultures, suspicion of Christianity as a politically destabilising factor, fear of losing one's cultural identity so closely related to millennia-old religions, emergence of governments of Socialist-Marxist ideological persuasion and Islamic fundamentalism have closed their doors to missionary work from outside Asia.[11]

The lesson is clear: Asians relating to their context in mission, in partnership and networking with the global church of Jesus Christ, are effective and responsible given the political and cultural realities. AMMs need to be equipped to take on the challenge to enter into a 'dialogue of life' with the culture and religions of Asia with a commitment to live the Good News in the ever changing cultural and religious milieu of Asia. We shall return to this later.

The Struggle for Cultural Identity

Confronted with modernity and ever stronger secularizing trends, Asian societies are threatened by the disintegration of traditional societies. In turn, serious

---

11   ibid, p. 53. The author, Sebastian Karotemprel goes on to assert that Fundamentalist Islamic governments of Pakistan, Bangladesh, Communist governments in Vietnam, Kampuchea, and China, strong Buddhist resistance to Christianity in Sri Lanka and Thailand make evangelization work almost impossible even by local churches in these countries. One may want to qualify and admit that there is (expatriate) missionary presence in these countries. The point is that if the Good News is to effectively permeate these countries without the burden of suspicion, apart from various other real challenges of cross-cultural missions, it can be done by local churches and believers.

challenges are raised against the cosmic worldview emanating from Asian religious cultures which view human beings, society and the whole universe holistically, as intimately related and interdependent.

There is bound to be a clash when spiritual values are persistently being replaced by the worship of technology through modernisation, more so when Asian societies get caught up in pursuit of materialism, secularism, consumerism and ideological pluralism. Global capitalism, spearheading industrialisation and urbanisation, almost consistently brings in its wake critical issues such as the exploitation of workers, widespread displacement including family break ups, and drugs and criminality among youth; the deprived and vulnerable are forced into cheap labour to survive. As 'market and money' assume control of Asian societies, for instance in Japan, (one of the world's least reached peoples) the business world comes to dominate the whole of society and social life. It absorbs the totality of people's lives. Individualism, consumerism and hedonism are reinforced. Community becomes less important, success in life is in the abundance of material possessions. Such disintegration of values creates crises in cultural identity.

Invariably the search for a sense of balance and harmony amid the rapid social changes and cultural confusion is what gives rise to fundamentalist sects with a strong emphasis on individualistic and spiritualistic notions. When these notions are wedded to political and communal motivations, they give rise to what is called 'traumatic pluralism'—religious fundamentalism of different shades that is quite strong in Asian societies today. "The revivalist religious movements exaggerate greatly the social, cultural and communalism side of one's religious adherence and try to exploit it for tangible economic and political gains."[12]

Can there ever be an articulation of a life affirming, relationally transforming, positively inclusive and compassionate spirituality without a real engagement with such cultural context of Asia? When AMMs begin to understand the Christian faith in terms of the life and needs of the Asia people from within, a living confession will develop which will try to relate the Biblical historical faith to contemporary Asia.

The Marginalised Poor

Some economists posit that there has been a steady decline in poverty in Asia over the past three decades as a direct result of the recent wave of globalization and the dynamic growth effect thereof. Yet more recently there is growing evidence that inequality has been rising. The rising inequalities in most developing Asian countries, it is argued, is the result of 'the rich getting richer faster than the poor' rather than 'the rich getting richer'.[13]

---

12   Pathil, K., *Mission in India*, Bangalore: Dharmaram Publications,1988), 138.

13   See an influential study, Machiko Nissanke and Eric Thorbecke (eds.) *Globalisation and the Poor in Asia: Can Shared Growth be Sustained* (Studies in Development Economics and Policy) Palgrave/Macmillan, 2008.

This is precisely the reason why there has to be a pro-poor approach in missions. In absolute numbers, Asia has the largest share of world's slum population, the direct result of rapid urbanisation. The structural imbalances in Asian societies make the vulnerable hapless victims of dehumanisation in the 'midst of plenty'. Millions live in near-genocidal squalor and appallingly poor sanitation facilities—described as the 'silent tsunami' in many Asian countries.

The Asia-Pacific region is home to nearly half the world's children, including large numbers of street children. According to the UNICEF, in 1998 there were about 25 million children estimated to be living on the streets in Asia. The child prostitution in every city of Asia, human migration and movement including the trafficking of children and young women across borders, the millions of children, elderly and single mothers roaming as beggars in the cities of Asia, the millions living their entire lives on the streets never to experience having a roof over their heads—this is also the world of Asia today, a continent of deep divisions, violence, sin and death.

The Church of the poor—the community of the Risen Lord—celebrates and witnesses to the reality of 'life in all its fullness' in the midst of sin and death. Herein lies the challenge of AMMs to declare the gospel in solidarity with the marginalised poor. AMMs along with the Church in the Majority World must continue to tap into the resources among the marginalised poor to be the authentic witnesses of transforming mission. This is 'Mission from the underside' (2 Cor. 8:9). Latin American and Asian liberation theologians will argue that the poor evangelises the rich; they are the agents to receive the Gospel, their continued struggles to overcome injustice and violence in the systems, sustains the momentum for Christian mission towards fullness of creation.[14]

Looking ahead in God's Mission in Asia

Crucial to our sustained efforts to equip and resource AMMs is the underlying premise that we remain sensitive to the Spirit to discern the major trends and challenges of Asia today—we are partners in the mission of God. We learn from the past and search for new paradigms for mission to encounter fresh challenges. In the following sections, we identify some of the considerations that are important for future mission and then move on to discuss ways and means of equipping ourselves.

A few guidelines to clarify directions for missions in Asia:[15]

14 Refer Huang Po Ho, "Doing Mission from the Underside - Mission Beyond Edinburgh 1910: Towards a Critical Asian Perspective", *theologies and cultures*, 2/5 December 2008, 37-61. Po Ho Huang is one of the leading theologians and a prolific writer from Taiwan. Asian Liberation theologians include Sebastian Kappen, Tissa Balasuriya and Carlos Abesamis.

15 James A. Scherer and Stephen B. Bevans, "Theological Foundations No.2," in *New Directions in Mission and Evangelization*, New York: Orbis, 1994, "Introduction," p.xi, as quoted by Sebastian Karotemprel (2000) op.cit., 51.

1. Culturally, politically, and economically today's world is pluricentric. In the years to come there is every indication that it will be even more so.

2. Religiously we live in a pluri-religious world.

3. There is a growing awareness and appreciation among Christians of the spiritual and soteriological values of other religions.

4. Involvement in the removal of structures of injustice and exploitation has become an essential element of Christian Mission and a matter of witness and credibility.

5. There is growing disenchantment with the capability of science, technology models of development today to solve the problems of humankind.

6. A new international order based upon Gospel and human values seems to be elusive. Interdependence of nations, cultures and even religions is on the increase.

7. Ecological problems call for the united efforts of peoples and religions.[16]

How then shall we equip and resource Missions?

Given the context of Asia, delineated in the preceding sections, with its unique challenges it is important that we consider the following:

16 Sebastian Karotemprel, (2000) op. cit. Compare Scherer-Bevans, " Basic Documents, No.1," in *New Directions in Mission and Evangelization*, New York: Orbis, 1992; David Bosch, *Transforming Mission: Paradigm Shifts in Theology of Mission*, New York: Orbis, 1991, especially "Mission in Many Modes", p.511-519.

'Mission is what happens when the church meets the world.' Preman Niles expands on this statement by the late Professor Feliciano Carino—"Mission is what happens at the places where the church meets the world, the world challenges the church, and the church responds creatively without simply reacting defensively."[17] Thus AMMs cannot be divorced from dialogue with the religious and cultural traditions of Asia; AMMs are called to discern/proclaim God's will within a pluralistic context. In any meaningful dialogue, each tradition is challenged to learn, unlearn and relearn; the only way the process becomes dynamic and mutually enriching.

In effect the challenge is to be authentic as AMMs assume the humble role of serving as the leaven and light among Asians with due respect to their religious convictions and cultural sensitivities. "In the Gospels we see that Jesus' mission was not so much to displace the religious roots of men and women as to deepen and enlarge their relationships, especially in so far as it involves their neighbour and God."[18]

Here is another vital element in the 'dialogue of life':

Without this continuing dialogue with God in Jesus Christ, Christian Mission will lose its moor-

17   D. Preman Niles, "Conformity and Contestation: An Asian Theological Appraisal of Edinburgh" *theologies and cultures*, 5/2 December 2008, 13.

18   Jacob Kavungal, "Asian Mission Theology: An Overview", in *Towards An Asian Theology of Mission*, Seigel and Mercado (eds). (1995).

ings and legitimacy. The evangeliser, even before dialogue with others, dialogues with Jesus Christ, his death- resurrection: If the dynamic of finding new life through death is the ultimate paradigm of Christian existence, then perhaps the death of Jesus is the key to a hermeneutic of Christian Mission in the contemporary world.[19]

'Missions from below': 'The Jesus way in bold humility'

Church history, thankfully, is more than Western missionary history. Mission history provides important insights regarding the dynamic of creativity within indigenous churches to achieve self identity and maturity in fulfilling God's mission in historical contexts. It is sustained through an ongoing process of identification; presumably aided by the 'Dialogue of life' as mentioned—enculturation—with realities such as the aspirations, feelings, thinking and cultures of the people. As C. S. Song puts it, "As we immerse ourselves in them, we touch the roots of our Asian being."[20] Mission in context is of the people, by the people and for the people. "Christianity is spread primarily by local believers and developed in local ways. Attention to the activities of foreign missionaries has tended to obscure this fact....that Christianity primarily spreads from below."[21]

Indigenous mission movements such as AMMs have a crucial role to foster missions from below involv-

19   William R. Burrows, ed. *Redemption and Dialogue*. New York: Orbis, 1993, p. 243, as quoted by Sebastian Kartomprel (2000), p. 51.

20   C. S. Song, "Christian Theology—Asian Way" *Tainan Theological Review* (1990), p. 124.

21   Kim, S. C. H and K. Kim, *Christianity as a World Religion*, London; Continuum, 2008, p. 211-212.

ing the 'ordinary'—women, young and the laity—so that the power and glory of God can flow through. This involves a departure from the 'missions of heroism' from above—with money, power, hierarchical leadership patterns, with control mechanisms and attitudes of moral superiority, and a belief in one's own exclusive righteousness. In sharp contrast, the Jesus Way in bold humility is one of strength perfected in weakness—mission in interdependence, meekness, patience, involving the costly movement outwards in self- giving love. This is applicable in situations where missionaries will have to learn to 'gracefully exit' handing over responsibility to local leaders as well as local leaders in Asia mentoring younger leaders to assume responsibility. Within the Asian culture there can be a cultural tendency of concentration of power and staying on in leadership.

Towards an ecumenical vision: mission spirituality in mutuality

In a Christian minority and multi-denominational context, ecumenical unity and co-operation is critical. Competition in missions is wasteful and self-defeating. "Learning from the past history ecumenism must not be just seen in functional terms but as a dynamic unity ('that they may be one')".[22] Huang from Taiwan insists, "Ecumenism is about a vision of God's household where the members seek to listen to the variety of Asian theological voices, and to practice intrafaith and

22   Wilfred J Samuel, *Review of the Critical Asian Principle (Malaysia, Thailand and Singapore Region)*, 2006, quoted by Po Ho Huang, op. cit, p. 60.

interfaith dialog in order to promote peace, healing and reconciliation."[23]

AMMs, like any other indigenous movements faces the real danger of becoming ethnocentric and must strive to avoid this by consistently affirming to 'act locally and think globally'—always fostering an ecumenical vision that would hold Christianity, West and East together. This was the clarion call in 1910 by a missionary statesman:

> It is in this co-operation of joint study at the feet of Christ that we shall realise the oneness of the Body of Christ. The exceeding riches of the glory of Christ can be fully realised not by the Englishman, the American, and the Continental alone, nor by the Japanese, the Chinese and the Indians by themselves—but by all working together, worshipping together, and learning together the Perfect Image of our Lord and Christ....We ought to be willing learn from one another and to help one another.[24]

Missions and money

As Asian economies assume greater autonomy and strength in the global market, mission movements in Asia must strive towards raising funds from within. The Asian diaspora can be motivated to resource local and missions abroad through AMMs. As Asia becomes financially more resourceful it is imperative that local Christians are challenged towards a robust spirituality

23   Po Ho Huang, p. 60.
24   V.S. Azariah in his presentation at the Edinburgh Conference 1910 – Refer *Edinburgh 1910 volume 9: The History and Records of the Conference: Together with Addresses delivered at the Evening Meetings,* London and Edinburgh: Oliphant, Anderson and Ferrier, exact publication date unknown, p.315.

inclusive of missional commitment and partnership, rather than an inward looking, simplistic spiritualism,

To cite just one example—there will be many others—indigenous mission agencies like the Friends Missionary Prayer Band, (FMPB) one of the largest mission movements in India, had from its inception a policy of not soliciting foreign funds for mission activities in India and neighbouring countries. The inflow of excessive foreign funds for mission in Asia can be counter productive; admittedly there is free flow of money for all religions today, and can bolster suspicions regarding the integrity of Christian missions. Accountability and stewardship of God's resources is also a powerful witness, more so in contexts where corruption is endemic.

Mission with the poor: Church of the poor

The poor shun abstract theology, and so should AMMs to equip themselves for the proclamation of the Gospel in solidarity with the poor in their struggle to realise their humanity, their human dignity. The poor find liberative motif in the 'Pain of God'. (Kosuke Koyama of Japan)

> In a country where poverty, deprivation and oppression are the common lot of the masses,... it is not surprising that the image the crucified one, head bowed, mouth agape in excruciating agony, provides consolation and an outlet for pent up emotions of sympathy and the tragedy for the ignorant and the heavy laden.[25]

25 Beltran, Benigno P. *The Christology of the Inarticulate: An Inquiry into the Filipino Understanding of Jesus Christ* (Manila: Divine World Publications, 1987), p. 123, as quoted by Jacob Kavungal, p. 99.

In most parts of Asia the struggle of the 'wretched of the earth'—the Minjung, Dalits, the urban/rural poor including women and children who are systematically exploited respond to the Gospel that affirms their humanity and self-worth in God. The struggles of the poor, a critical reality of Asia, reflect the basic search for human dignity and justice.

Abesamis, a Filipino theologian insists that the concept of salvation that has become individualistic, dualistic and other worldly under the impact of Greek philosophy is not biblical.

> It is today's poor and their struggle that have challenged us to go back to our biblical roots and rediscover the gospel of justice, and liberation in the very core of Jesus' original mission. May this gospel in turn help to free us to dedicate ourselves to the task of justice and liberation in our time.[26]

The vast majority of poor in Asia, be it the tribals, adivasis—the indigenous peoples, 'the little ones—insignificant and overlooked' breaking free from the shackles of oppression and realising their potential in a loving God—'a no-people becoming the people of God' (indigenous movements)—is the greatest resource for God's mission in the multi-cultural context of Asia. Such mission from below brings a radical shift in which the agency of mission is replaced from the rich to the poor—true people's movement rather than missions being the exclusive arena for the resourceful experts, specialists and the qualified.

26 Abesamis, Carlos. *Religion and Society*, Manila, 1987, p. 213, quoted by Jacob Kavungal.

Missions and women

Even though women form a large percentage of the poor, their contributions in the home and the informal sectors produce and sustain life. Globally women have been great witnesses in affirming life and justice; even so gender injustices imposed by patriarchal culture of domination and subordination are a real challenge and militates against efforts towards an inclusive, just society. In articulating visions and working towards the reality of social structures based on mutuality and participation, women's perspectives and insights are fundamental. Their perspectives are critical in redefining missions from the point of view of those who suffer systemic violence and long for a gender-just relational spirituality.

Missions and ecological concerns

With huge challenges of ecology—a matter of life and death in many parts of Asia, and affecting every part of the world today, this becomes an area of huge importance for Asian missions. Today, missions with an anthropocentric soteriology, another offshoot of dualistic reasoning, is found seriously wanting; care for nature is an integral part of the holistic vision of Shalom. The devastations brought about by ecological imbalances have highlighted the dangers of a flawed understanding of development with sinful tendencies towards accumulation and indiscriminate use of resources. Care and concern for nature is borne out of a theology and practice of missions with an emphasis on the communality and interrelatedness of creation.

AMMs set as they are within the complex and critical realities of the context in 'times such as these',—a creative missional minority in the midst of massive poverty and of richness of religions and culture- are confronted with a gospel mandate to equip itself through a sustained dialogue of life with religion, culture and the disenfranchised poor. Such a creative encounter of Gospel and culture reinforces the impetus for relevant mission paradigms that are transformational.

The resourcing of Christian mission in Asia is primarily through 'missions from the underside'—mission through God's 'ordinary' yet committed disciples—children, men, women and youth of Asia, in partnership with God and fellow pilgrims of the global church, who are not only bearers of the good news but embodying in integrity and faithful obedience a spirituality of radical love and mutuality that is truly liberating, inclusive and counter cultural, '... not with wise and persuasive words, but with a demonstration of the Spirit's power....' (1 Cor. 2:4, NIV)

> "In many places of the world the departures of missionaries have given the indigenous churches an important evangelistic impetus."[27]

Dr Jacob Thomas is Lecturer in Missiology at Belfast Bible College.

---

27   Hollenwerger ,Walter, J. "My Pilgrimage in Mission", *International Bulletin of Missionary Research* 29/2 (2005), p. 87.

Resourcing and Developing Christian Apologetics in South Asia

Exploring sustainable resourcing of indigenous and emerging Asian mission movements and the potential for partnerships

Asif Mall

Why is Christian Apologetics Necessary in South Asia?

Apologetics and polemics are deeply ingrained in the very psyche, tradition and culture of South Asians in general, particularly amongst those who adhere to the religion of Islam. As a South Asian from Pakistan, I can say that we South Asians have the Athenian syndrome, which is to discuss new ideas about everything, especially about faith issues. The dynamics of these discussions change and vary, depending upon whether the discussion is in relation to inclusive religions like Hinduism and Buddhism, or some exclusive religions like Judaism, Christianity and Islam. The way Christian apologetics is used in relation to Hinduism would be quite different from when it is applied during dialogue with Islam, though primarily the underlying Biblical principle would stay the same.

The inclusive nature of Hinduism, Sikhism, Jainism and Buddhism means that they do not seem to have the same wavelength of polemics against Christianity as Islam. A Hindu does not have much of a problem in accepting Jesus as God, as it is a matter of adding Jesus to the 160 million Hindu gods; they might even tell you that you can be a Hindu and a Christian at the same time. For a Buddhist, there is no dichotomy in being a Christian and a Buddhist at the same time; because Buddha is a stage of enlightenment and they are happy to accept Jesus as one of their Buddhas. Because of their inclusive nature, these religions are not as evangelistic as Christianity and Islam, and definitely not as polemical towards Christianity as Islam.

Both Christianity and Islam are very exclusive faiths, with very little if at all any grey areas. You are either in or you are out! If you profess to be a Christian or a Muslim, then you cannot be something else at the same time. Gnostics tried syncretising Christianity with pantheism, but they failed; similar efforts for syncretising Islam were made by the Mughal emperor, Jalal-ul-Din Akbar, but they were not successful either. Today we read about Gnosticism and Akbar's Deen-e-Elahi only in history books, as neither of them have any known followers.

Both Christianity & Islam claim to have the ultimate truth, which makes them inherently evangelistic in nature, as they both feel that it is their duty to propagate and defend their God given truth. This kind of exclusivity combined with a divine evangelistic mandate often brings the both religions into confrontation all over the world and South Asia is no exception in this matter. During the last couple of hundred years, South Asia has seen many Muslim polemicists, who have mainly targeted Christianity in their effort to try to make Islam win by default. It is not surprising at all that most of the Christian apologetics in South Asia have also been focussed mainly on answering the Muslim objections to Christianity. For this reason, as we discuss about Christian apologetics in South Asia, the main thrust of our focus in this paper will stay on Christian Muslim apologetics.

When we think of the South Asian Muslim polemics in the last hundred years, then two names immediately come to mind. They are Ahmed Deedat and Dr. Zakir Naik, both of them famous for their debates with known Christian apologists. A brief examination of their life and works will help us to comprehend the need for Christian Apologetics in the South Asian context.

Ahmed Deedat was from South Asian (Indian) background, but born and raised in South Africa (1918-2005). He wrote a lot of polemical material in the late 20th century, including many books, which are very popular amongst South Asian Muslims all over the world. These books raise many questions about the fundamental beliefs and tenets of the Christian faith, hence challenging the very foundations of our Christian faith. The titles of some of his books are self explanatory as to their content, such as:

- Is the Bible God's Word?

- What The Bible Says About Muhammad

- Crucifixion or Cruci-Fiction?

- Muhammad: The Natural Successor to Christ

- Christ in Islam, Muhammad The Greatest

- Al-Qur'an the Miracle of Miracles.

Saudi Arabia generously gave money for the printing of a collated volume of four of Deedat's popular booklets titled "The Choice: Islam and Christianity", and the entire book is also available on the Internet. The extreme polemics used by Deedat in his debates with Christians inspired many Muslims worldwide and we still see the resonance of his arguments during discussion between Muslims and Christians today.

Dr. Zakir Naik was born in India in 1965, he claims to have been inspired by the late Ahmed Deedat and seems to copy the Deedat style while debating Christians. Dr. Naik is the founder and president of the Islamic Research Foundation (IRF) and he owns the global "Peace TV", which is watched by millions of Muslims all over the world. He has a remarkable ability to memorise a large number of Biblical, Koranic and Hadith references, and Anthropologist Thomas Blom Hansen has written that Naik's style of memorizing the Qur'an and Hadith literature in various languages and related missionary activity has made him extremely popular in Muslim and non-Muslim circles.

The books written by both Deedat and Naik are widely available in South Asia and at Muslims book stores around the world. The CDs and DVDs of their lectures and debates are being distributed by Islamic centres and mosques around the world.

What has already been done and achieved?

Christian apologetics in South Asia also has a history of over a hundred years and it seems to have flourished substantially during the British colonial time. Most of the Christian apologetics in South Asia have been focussed on responding to the Muslim and Ahmadi polemics, because they are the two main groups raising objections about the Christian faith. Some of these Christian apologetics materials were also written for the purpose of propagating and not merely defending the Christian faith.

A few prominent Christian apologists during British Raj in South Asia are Bishop Karl Pfander, Maulvi Pardi Abdul Haq, Maulana Sultan Mohammad Paul, Allama Barkat Ullah, Akbar Masih, Edward Canon Sell, G.L. Thakar Dass, Barkat A. Khan, Maulvi Hashmat Ullah and Imad-ud-Din Lahzer. The books written by these apologists are part of the remarkable legacy of Christian apologetics in South Asia. The Pakistan Government has banned all of these books, as the apologetics content is deemed to be a threat to Islam. Therefore these books are not available at any bookshops in Pakistan, though a lot of these books in the Urdu language are being made available on the internet.

Despite such a rich heritage of Christian apologetics in South Asia, no notable new material has been written since 1947, the year when India and Pakistan became independent nations. After independence, Indian Christians did not feel the need to produce any Christian-Muslim apologetics, their context being a Hindu majority nation; whereas in Pakistan the subsequent Governments made it difficult for Pakistani Christians to produce any material on this subject. The draconian Blasphemy Laws in Pakistan make it even harder to write apologetics materials in Pakistan, as section 295-C of the Pakistan Penal Code carries a mandatory death sentence for anyone deemed to be insulting Islam. Even if anyone writes any fresh apologetics materials, then it is difficult to surmount the challenge of getting it published, as most publishers in Pakistan won't even touch such material due to fear for their lives.

The challenges of producing fresh apologetics materials has resulted in magnifying the value of the existing writings of Christian apologists from the colonial time, as that is the best that is available to the church in South Asia. Even though these materials are still very useful, there is an urgent need for producing fresh materials for responding to the contemporary challenges posed by a new generation of Muslim polemicists.

What is God already doing?

God has prompted churches, ministries and individuals to advance the Kingdom in South Asia through the usage of Christian apologetics. Ravi Zacharias Ministry has been offering up to one year of training in apologetics and evangelism in India, whereas various correspondence courses in Christian apologetics are also available.

In Pakistan, New Life Institute and The Christian Theological Research Centre are helping believers learn about Christian apologetics. Bible colleges in Pakistan are trying to develop the module of apologetics for their students, as they are increasingly becoming convinced that the future of the Church in Pakistan depends upon the ability of the pew sitters to be able to give a reason for their faith in Jesus Christ. During an evangelistic media consultation in Pakistan in 2009, it was decided to have a network of Christian apologists in Pakistan, committed to developing and identifying fresh apologetics materials for making them available to Churches in Pakistan.

A somewhat similar initiation is underway in Bangladesh, where a lot of apologetics materials are being produced in Bengali and English language to make them available to churches through the internet. One can hope that some of these initiatives in Pakistan, India and Bangladesh will have ripple effects in the neighbouring South Asian nations like, Nepal, Bhutan, Sri Lanka and Maldives.

The Potential, Scope & Need for Developing Fresh Apologetics Approaches

The church in South Asia needs to develop its own South Asian paradigms for Christian apologetics, which can strike chords with the mindset and worldview of the South Asians. There is indeed room for translating some of the excellent books written by Western Christian apologists, but South Asian apologists would still need to develop ways to contextualise that knowledge to maximise its benefits for the church in that part of the world. For example, political correctness is considered a virtue in the Western world, but that would be taken as a sign of weakness while defending the Gospel in South Asia because the perception is that if one claims to have the truth, then they must be able to present it in an unapologetic and straightforward manner.

New paradigms for apologetics should also be explored, especially in the context of Christian Muslim apologetics in South Asia. It seems that Muslim polemicists make Christian apologists dance to their tune, making Christians defend whatever Muslims want them to defend, not necessarily what should be defended. For example Muslim polemicists would say that Jesus is not the son of God and he did not die on the cross, and Christian apologist would immediately start giving reasons from the Bible to prove the deity of Christ, his death and resurrection. After the Christian apologist is exhausted with trying to establish the deity, death and resurrection of Christ in the Bible, the Muslim polemicist would simply turn around and say that since the Bible has been corrupted and hence is unreliable, why should he believe anything Christians quote from the Bible? The Christian apologist would then wholeheartedly start giving reasons to prove that the Bible is trustworthy, only to have the Muslim polemicist object to the Trinity, and here we go again. The worst aspect of such encounters is that we often get so carried away with defending what we are forced to defend, that we almost forget to present the gospel.

Instead of indulging in these knee jerk reactions with Muslims and calling it apologetics, we need to think more carefully about what is so unique and special about the Christian faith, and how we can best present and defend it. We need to diligently craft our methodologies for effectively presenting the gospel, because our apologetics are worthless if not helping us in our primary task of sharing the good news. Christian apologists should always keep their eyes on the ball that the Gospel message needs to be shared no matter what, instead of being carried away with the fervour of trying to respond to red herrings, which are often meant to create the smoke screen in which the message of the gospel is lost. In my opinion, none of the above Muslim arguments is a primary argument; as all of them are like the branches of a tree and not the trunk, and however many branches we cut, the new ones always keep growing.

Most of the Muslim polemics against the Bible are primarily based on the Koranic view that God is basically in the business of giving guidance to humankind through books and prophets, i.e. he sent Moses with the Old Testament, Jesus with the New Testament and Mohammad with the Last Testament, and since the Koran is the Last and Final Testament, it is superior to both the Old and New Testaments, because it is like a guardian that identifies and corrects the mistakes made in both the previous Testaments.

When we examine the Muslim objections to Christianity in the light of the above supposition, it gives us a deeper insight into the Muslim mindset. We start to comprehend the reasoning behind their arguments against the trinity, the deity of Christ and his death and resurrection. Christian apologists need to realise that it does not matter how much evidence they produce from the Bible or how eloquently it is presented because if it fails to engage and respond to the above Koranic supposition, it makes little or no sense to them. Christian apologists need to produce a convincing defence of the New Testament to be the Final Testament from God, as that is the only sure way of tackling the above Islamic perception; otherwise our apologetics will continue to be like fighting with a squid with a thousand tentacles, as no matter how many tentacles you chop you will never win if are not trying to reach for its head.

Christians need to understand that we are people of the covenant, because the God of the Bible is inherently a God of covenants. A testament is merely a written record of a covenant, which is meant to testify to the covenant between two individuals or groups. A marriage certificate is a testament of a marital covenant between a man and a woman, as it testifies to the covenant taken by them to become husband and wife. The Old and New Testaments in the Bible are the written records, testifying to various covenants between God and humanity. The Koran refers to Jews and Christians as *Ahle-Kitab* (people of the book), but we need to gently remind them that first and foremost we are a people of the covenant and then a people of the book. As marriage is more important than the marriage certificate; in the same way God's covenants are more important than the testaments, which are merely written records, testifying to those covenants.

Muslim polemicists are very keen to compare the Old and New Testaments to the Koran, allegedly the last testament of God, and they like to point out all sorts of alleged contradictions, corruptions and changes in the Bible to demonstrate that Koran is superior to the Bible. Christian apologists have danced long enough to this tune for the last fourteen hundred years of Islam. I believe that we should start to engage our Muslim friends in comparing Biblical covenants with the alleged Islamic covenant, which Muslims claim the Koran testifies to as the Last and Final Testament. We also need to equip Christians in South Asia and elsewhere into analytical thinking, hence enabling them to rediscover aspects of our scriptures which can be powerful tools for presenting and defending the Gospel. Being people of God's covenants, we will also need to explore ways of dwelling on the covenants between us and God, as this will surely enable us as we propagate and defend the gospel in ways more powerful than we can imagine in living memory.

Partnerships for Resourcing South Asian Churches with Apologetics

Partnerships can be a complicated phenomenon and a huge amount of trust is needed on both sides for making it work. As churches and mission organisations in the West seek to resource South Asian indigenous church planting movements to help them develop effective apologetics in advancing the Lord's Kingdom in South Asia, it will be a blessed experience for all parties. I would like to identify a few areas with an urgent need for developing such partnerships:

Modules of Christian apologetics for Bible Colleges and Seminaries in South Asia.

Extensive Apologetics training for lay Christians. Supporting the national apologists.

Help with the publication of new materials.

Scholarships for outstanding South Asian apologists.

Dissemination through Internet, Radio and Satellite TV.

Most of the theological seminaries and Bible colleges in South Asia, particularly in countries like Pakistan and Bangladesh, do not even have a module for Christian apologetics. They have hardly any books on Christian apologetics in their libraries, let alone the latest materials on this subject. Modules for Christian apologetics should be introduced at certificate, diploma and degree levels in some of these South Asian seminaries and Bible colleges; they should even be affiliated with some of the known seminaries and Bible colleges in the Western world. Funding should be sought to help purchase apologetics related books for the libraries of these seminaries, enabling them to have the latest books on apologetics for equipping the future generations of Christians in South Asia, as it is crucial for the survival and growth of the church in that part of the word.

Most of the seminaries in South Asia are very focussed on preparing people for ordained pastoral ministry and they have hardly anything on offer to lay Christians. I believe that a 1-5 week long extensive residential training in Christian apologetics should also be offered for lay Christians, similar to the one offered by the RZIM summer school. The lay Christians are more likely to come across people of other faiths at their work places and such investment into their lives will enable them to become confident Christians and better witnesses for the gospel.

Most of the Christian apologists in South Asia are in full time secular jobs to earn bread and butter for themselves and their families. Some of them can be supported to be released to spend more time, if not full time, to develop and formalise their research and be able to teach it to equip local churches. Some of the Western Mission organisations working in South Asia can employ some of these apologists, thus enabling them to fulfil their God given calling and vision. A number of apologists have written good books, booklets and pamphlets, but resources were not available to get them printed. Some assistance for the publication of outstanding works can be a way to bless churches in these South Asian nations. Already existing forums and networks of Christian apologists in South Asia can help identify and recommend apologetics materials, and the funding should be granted for the publications of these materials for equipping the church for presenting and defending the gospel. Investment into the research done by South Asian apologists into various aspects of Christian apologetics is eventually going to be useful for the Church in the West as it responds to the challenge of Islam and other religious movements within Europe and North America.

A scholarship fund can also be established to enable some of the emerging South Asian apologists to carry out further research at the Bible colleges in the Western world. This should also be seen as an investment towards the growth and strengthening of the South Asian apologetics based evangelistic movements.

Currently there are various Internet related evangelistic projects that are underway in South Asia. The Internet is a very powerful medium, which is being used by more and more South Asians every day. This provides Christians with a phenomenal opportunity to propagate the gospel to a very large number of people in South Asia, especially the relatively closed nations like Maldives and Bhutan or the restricted nations like, Pakistan, Bangladesh and Nepal. India and Sri Lanka are relatively open countries, so the opportunities for proclaiming the gospel through the Internet are even greater.

Satellite TV channels are a relatively recent phenomenon, but one of the fastest growing ones. It seems that more and more satellite channels are starting in the world and South Asia is no exception. A lot of these satellite channels are offering entertainment, sports and news; but there are many Islamic, Hindu and Sikh Satellite TV channels, which are propagating these religions in various South Asian languages. A number of Christian satellite channels are also busy propagating the gospel in Arabic and Farsi languages, but unfortunately to date there is no Christian satellite TV channel to broadcast the good news in South Asia in Urdu, Hindi, Punjabi, Guajarati and other South Asian languages. Starting a satellite TV channel is a costly business, but Churches in the West should prayerfully consider partnering with the South Asian church movements to start such TV channels, because these channels have the potential to reach more people than we can count.

When we talk about apologetics based South Asian church planting movements, let us not forget nearly

3 million South Asians in the UK and a much larger number of them throughout Western Europe. These South Asians living in UK, Europe, North America and Australia probably surf the web and watch Satellite TV channels more than the South Asians living in South Asia, which is a huge God given opportunity to reach them with the gospel, though sadly most of it is being missed by the church. There are 19 UK based satellite channels that are run by Muslims, 6 run by Hindus and 2 run by Sikhs and one run by the Buddhists; providing religious programmes in English and South Asian languages. There are currently a wide range of US based Christian channels, and some African ones which somehow do not tend to appeal to South Asian viewers due to linguistic and cultural barriers. There is currently only one Christian channel that is presenting the Gospel in South Asian languages to viewers in the UK and Europe, but it is very lopsided, as most of the focus is on India and very little is being done in terms of apologetics-based evangelistic programmes for South Asian Muslims. There is an opportunity for partnership between Western churches and South Asian Christian apologists in the UK to initiate a UK based Satellite TV channel, to preach the gospel to

South Asians not only in South Asian but throughout the world.

These are many more areas of mission, evangelism and training where all sorts of other gospel partnerships can be forged between emerging mission movements in South Asia and the established churches in the Western world. Due to the limitations of this paper, only some of the more significant and urgent opportunities for partnership are discussed and it is sincerely believed that the results would be beneficial for the strengthening and growth of the church not only in South Asia, but also in many other parts of the world.

Asif Mall is a Christian apologist and an evangelist from Pakistan, working in the UK.

Concern For The City

Florence Tan

The Bible records in Micah 6:9a that "the LORD's voice cries to the city" declaring punishment for injustice. Jesus wept for His city, Jerusalem. He loved the people, even the Pharisees, and reached out to them with His mother-love image as portrayed in Matthew 23:37-39, speaking pointedly so that the hearers would choose to receive or reject His outstretched hand.[1] He talked to the cities: Chorazin, Capernaum, Bethsaida, Tyre and Sidon.

God's heart had always been for the inhabitants of urbanised localities with all their cultural and religious plurality and exclusiveness existing side by side,[2] immorality and idolatry. He would be mindful of that one faithful soul in Sodom. He ensured that the thousands in Nineveh got the good news from Jonah. Therefore, just as a pastor is directed to serve in a particular church, a missionary to an unreached people group, so an individual with evangelistic objectives can fulfil a mission in a certain city to which God might lead.

---

1   Green, Michael, *The Message of Matthew.* Leicester, UK: Inter-Varsity Press, 2000, p. 247.

2   Michael Pocock, "Intercultural Ministry in Culturally Diverse Communities: The compass for the Journey" in Florence Tan, ed. *Missions Matrix: Navigating 21C Missiological Issues*, Singapore: Singapore Bible College, 2007, p. 16.

Antioch in Syria was a significant city during the first century AD. A focal point of trade and industry, it was one of the places that people of multi-faith gathered. After Stephen's death, persecuted followers of Jesus Christ made their way to Antioch as well as other areas around and beyond Phoenicia, like Cyprus. The gospel was preached and well received, as mentioned in Acts 11:21.

The leadership at Jerusalem sent Barnabas to check on the Antiochan church; he ended up encouraging the healthy growing group of believers known for their social concern. He later invited Saul to join him in strengthening the flourishing congregation. It was a good training ground for the latter, who, together with his mentor, stayed on a full year engaged in the disciple-making ministry. Antioch earned the status of being the mother of Gentile churches, as Christians there proclaimed unreservedly, "Jesus is Lord."[3] This unique city also excelled in becoming a solid missionary-sending base claiming Barnabas and Saul (later renamed Paul) as their famous missionaries, the first mobile church-planting team. This called and confirmed pair was commissioned by the Spirit in an era uncomplicated by church rules and mission agency regulations.

For these postmodern days, Ortiz suggests multiple church models when ministering to city folk, since the populated locale is not static but is usually in a state

3   Roger S. Greenway, "Antioch: A Biblical Model of Urban Church Development" in Greenway & Monsma, eds., *Cities: Missions' New Frontiers*, Grand Rapids, MI: Baker Books, 1989, p.57.

of flux. He offers images of the prophet, priest and pilgrim to describe the holistic function of church as the new community.[4] The church exhibits her prophetic side in speaking out against sin and social injustices; performs the duties of the priest in bringing needy and hurting hearts to God for salvation and healing; and motivates each one in the journey through different phases of life. Missiological education therefore cannot escape from some degree of consideration of urban priority areas, of quality of life, health and community development for the homeless, handicapped, helpless and hopeless.[5]

What then can the simple average sincere evangelistic Christian do in the face of such giant needs-where to draw the balance of dishing out the spiritual food of the gospel and presenting a hearty meal to feed a hungry soul?[6]

The Asian situation

Population growth has so accelerated that it is extrapolated that a billion people will be added in the present decade. These explosive numbers are found in Asia, which implies that urbanising is parallel to asianising, most obviously in the Pacific Rim region.[7]

4   Manuel Ortiz, "The Church and the City" in Manuel and Baker, eds., *The Urban Face of Mission : Ministering the Gospel in a Diverse and Changing World*, Phillipsburg, NJ: P & R Publishing Co., 2002, p.58.
5   Andrew Kirk, "A Different Task: Liberation Theology and Local Theologies" in Anthony Harvey, ed., *Theology in the City : A Theological Response to "Faith in the City"*, London: SPCK, 1989, p. 30.
6   For a more elucidate discussion read Ha, Janice. "Stepping into Evangelism-Centred Social Action in Missions" in Florence Tan, ed. *Creative Crossings: Navigating 21st Century Contextualisation*, pp. 1-30.
7   Bakke, Ray. *A Theology as Big as the City*, Downers Grove, IL: InterVarsity Press, 1997, p. 13.

It has been observed that mushrooming city-states were the result of a few major developments like the collapse of political blocks and post-colonialism, massive migration, electronic media, and prompt recovery from economic crisis.[8] For example, the UK newspaper The Times reported that 1 million moved from Malaysia to Singapore during the period of 1960-2005.[9] According to Mahbubani, "billions of Asians are marching to modernity."[10]

Singapore is strategically located among the dynamic economies of the Pacific Rim. Blair has placed high expectations on this "little red dot," being a microcosm of globalisation with a melting pot of different cultures, major commercial links and positioned as a hub for Southeast Asia and Australasia.[11] What Antioch did for the Roman Empire in de-Judaising Christianity, perhaps Singapore can do in de-westernising Christianity for the unreached peoples of Asia?[12]

It is ironic to think that the world entering the twenty-first century with a strong sense of utopia would have a premonition of doom and gloom. Many among secular observers anticipate in decades to come, colossal calamities in the form of environmental catastrophe and major governmental policy failures

8   Anthony D. King, "Cities: Contradictory Utopias" in Pieterse, Jan Nederveen, ed., *Global Futures: Shaping Globalisation*, NY: Zed Books Ltd., 2000, pp 234-235.
9   The Times (UK) Tuesday, September 22, 2009: p. 28.
10   Mahbubani, Kishore. *The New Asian Hemisphere: The Irresistible Shift of Global Power to the East*, NY: PublicAffairs, 2008, p.3.
11   The Straits Times, Friday, August 14, 2009: A24.
12   Edward K. Pousson, "Are we Antioch yet?" in Catalyse, Singapore Centre for Evangelism and Missions 2008/03: pp 1,2.

perhaps necessitating a one-world government.[13] Is this not reminiscent of the drama vividly and prophetically portrayed in Revelation 13?

Bible-believing people will not sit idly by, waiting for the worst to happen. Mission-minded Christ's disciples with conviction in their heads, compassion in their hearts are committed to work with their hands, according to appropriate skills and gifting, to do that which is possible to fulfil Christ's Great Commission.

Participation and witness

Today many in Singapore are motivated to participate, which leads some to wonder whether this cosmopolitan city-state is indeed the modern Antioch of Asia in terms of missionary effort. With an annual rate of 8.6% over 30 years of Gross National Income,[14] this island nation has already gained first-world status. With mega-churches sprouting, she has the necessary human and financial resources[15] to bless her neighbours and people far beyond her shores.

Networks of "primary" relationships can be biological, geographical, vocational or recreational in nature.[16] Workers identify themselves through the type of jobs they do. It becomes natural for likeminded persons to be found together. The cab-drivers in Southeast Asian cities can be engaged in interesting

13   Clifford Hill, *Shaking the Nations : A Future and a Hope*. E. Essex: Kingsway Publications Ltd., 1995, p. 202.

14   Mahbubani, p. 54.

15   http://forums.vr-zone.com/newsroom/412622-news-sgd500k-salary-singapore-new-creation- church-leader.html

16   Bakke, Ray with Jim Hart, *The Urban Christian*, Downers Grove, IL: InterVarsity, 1987.

hot topics during their break at the favourite coffee shop. The soccer or rugby-mad kids would kick around or rough it out whenever there is free time. Girls love to be together going through their favourite songs or being engaged in fashion talk. The computer geeks and gaming addicts will be lost in cyberspace most of the time. It is no wonder then that nowadays "cold calling" evangelism will result in extremely little or no response.

How shall the pre-believers hear if no one is on hand to tell (Romans 11:14)? Those with hearts of compassion for the lost have tried (Romans 11:15) and they have succeeded through the blessings of conversion by the Holy Spirit. Using a medium-sized (2,000) intentional disciple-making church in Singapore as an example, here is some feedback.

Conversions were registered through the ALPHA programme, cell-group outreach and personal witnessing. Many evangelistic efforts (peppered with prayer) were tried, such as block blessing,[17] meals-on-wheels, movie-showing, festivals (cultural or national in nature) events, kids-for-Christ (KFC) activities, youth-biking sport, senior line-dancing, tours around the island and overseas. Several groups of church members made short-term mission trips to poor areas to serve (feed and clean), teach (simple English and Bible) or build or repair (paths, lean-to sheds, furniture, etc.). Other practical forms of social action included dispensing medicine and offering dental care or initiating faith gardens. They contacted their own

17   On a designated Sunday, Christians bring fruits or bread to each household/unit in apartment blocks of ten or more storeys high to bless them and invite them to a carnival with free coupons .

home-grown missionaries as well, to encourage and join in ministry events during quick or spontaneous visits.

If mission-conscious believers are not venturing out, they can do as much, if not more, while remaining in their respective countries. These local tentmakers, the self-supporting professionals do go "glocal"—having, and functioning with, a global mindset while staying-put on home ground most of the time, traversing the planet when necessary. Such a cohort has the means to be efficient with their financial resources and definitely effective when devoted to God's overall grand goals in making disciples.

Midge of Malaysia had been a faithful witness since her university days in the capital city. Many individuals especially colleagues, in both cities where she worked testified to her gentle ways, sincere friendship and simple, inoffensive sharing of the gospel and had been won over to the Lord Jesus Christ. Even now as a retiree, she continues to be gainfully employed and firmly entrenched in her commitment to be involved in evangelising ("going"), establishing ("baptising") and equipping ("teaching") as spelled out in the Great Commission (Matthew 28:18-20).

Conclusion

With God everything is possible (Luke 1:37). The city may be large with numerous distractions. Amidst the bustling crowd, Jesus commended the faith of the Syro-Phoenician woman who did not mind the crumbs meant for little dogs. It really does not matter whether it is to the uneducated or under-dressed person that we are communicating with, or hobnobbing with the sophisticated fashionable well-bred in the city, ambassadors for Christ are to be ready with the answer of the reason of the hope that we have in Christ (1 Peter 3:15). Gone are the days of simple ready-made answers. Well-thought through arguments are preferred by searching intellectuals.

And as Joon-Sik Park puts it, "Authentic evangelism is deeply dependent on genuine hospitality."[18]

Dr Florence Poh-Lian Tan is Former Lecturer and Director of Field Education, Singapore Bible College

18   Park, Joon-Sik. "Hospitality as Context for Evangelism," *Missiology* 30:3 (July 2002), p.389.